THE FIRST EMPEROR

SIMA QIAN's *Historical Records* (*Shiji*), from which this selection is taken, is the most famous Chinese historical work, which not only established a pattern for later Chinese historical writing, but was also much admired for its literary qualities, not only in China, but also in Japan, where it became available as early as the eighth century AD. The work is vast and complex, and to appreciate its nature it is necessary to make a selection of passages concerning a particular period. To this end the short-lived Qin Dynasty, which unified China in the late third century BC, has been chosen for this translation as a key historical period which well illustrates Sima's method. Sima himself lived from 145 BC to about 86 BC. He inherited the post of Grand Historiographer from his father, and was so determined to complete his work that he suffered the penalty of castration rather than the more honourable alternative of death when he fell foul of the Emperor.

RAYMOND DAWSON was an Emeritus Fellow of Wadham College, Oxford. He was Editor of *The Legacy of China* (1964) and his other publications include *The Chinese Chameleon: An Analysis of European Conceptions of Chinese Civilization* (1967), *Imperial China* (1972), *The Chinese Experience* (1978), *Confucius* (1982), *A New Introduction to Classical Chinese* (1984), and the *Analects* (Oxford World's Classics, 1993).

K. E. BRASHIER is Associate Professor of Religion (Chinese) and Humanities (Chinese) at Reed College.

OXFORD WORLD'S CLASSICS

*For over 100 years Oxford World's Classics have brought
readers closer to the world's great literature. Now with over 700
titles—from the 4,000-year-old myths of Mesopotamia to the
twentieth century's greatest novels—the series makes available
lesser-known as well as celebrated writing.*

*The pocket-sized hardbacks of the early years contained
introductions by Virginia Woolf, T. S. Eliot, Graham Greene,
and other literary figures which enriched the experience of reading.
Today the series is recognized for its fine scholarship and
reliability in texts that span world literature, drama and poetry,
religion, philosophy and politics. Each edition includes perceptive
commentary and essential background information to meet the
changing needs of readers.*

OXFORD WORLD'S CLASSICS

——

SIMA QIAN

The First Emperor

Selections from the
Historical Records

——

Translated with an Introduction and Notes by
RAYMOND DAWSON

Preface by
K. E. BRASHIER

OXFORD
UNIVERSITY PRESS

OXFORD

UNIVERSITY PRESS

Great Clarendon Street, Oxford OX2 6DP

Oxford University Press is a department of the University of Oxford.
It furthers the University's objective of excellence in research, scholarship,
and education by publishing worldwide in

Oxford New York

Auckland Cape Town Dar es Salaam Hong Kong Karachi
Kuala Lumpur Madrid Melbourne Mexico City Nairobi
New Delhi Shanghai Taipei Toronto

With offices in

Argentina Austria Brazil Chile Czech Republic France Greece
Guatemala Hungary Italy Japan Poland Portugal Singapore
South Korea Switzerland Thailand Turkey Ukraine Vietnam

Oxford is a registered trade mark of Oxford University Press
in the UK and in certain other countries

Published in the United States
by Oxford University Press Inc., New York

First published (as *Historical Records*) as a World's Classics paperback 1994
Published as an Oxford World's Classics paperback, with new Preface by
K. E. Brashier, 2007
Reissued 2009

British Library Cataloguing in Publication Data

Data available

Library of Congress Cataloging in Publication Data

Sima, Qian. ca. 145–ca. 86 B.C.
[Shi ji. English Selections]
The first emperor : selections from the Historical Records / translated with an
introduction and notes by Richard Dawson : preface by K. E. Brashier.
p. cm. – (Oxford world's classics)
Includes bibliographical references and index.
ISBN 978–0–19–957439–1 (alk. paper)
1. Qin shi huang, Emperor of China, 259–210 B.C. 2. China — History — Qin
dynasty, 221–207 B.C. 3. China — kings and rulers — Biography. I. Dawson,
Raymond Stanley. II. Title.
DS747.9.Q254S56 2007
931'.04092 — dc22
[B]
2007007676

ISBN 978–0–19–957439–1

1

Typeset by Cepha Imaging Private Ltd., Bangalore, India
Printed in Great Britain
on acid-free paper by
Clays Ltd, St Ives plc

CONTENTS

PREFACE
VIEWS OF THE FIRST EMPEROR

Our modern era regards the First Emperor as the glue that brought Chinese culture together in terms of territory, currency, measures, roads, written language and more. Books and documentaries routinely dub him 'the man who made China', elevating him to creator status. Images of his cruelty may persist, but the warfare, the quest for immortality, and his exacting laws are now often treated as necessary evils and personal quirks leading to the much greater prize of unification, of fusing 'all under Heaven' or *tianxia*.

We see the First Emperor of Qin through several different lenses. First, there is the self-projected image of the Qin ruler, an image now being reconstructed through the things he left behind, ranging from terracotta warriors to mountain inscriptions. Second, there is the lens polished by Sima Qian, the Grand Historiographer who lived a century after the First Emperor. For him, the First Emperor wasn't the founder of an imperial tradition that would last two thousand years; he was the unpopular Qin opportunist from a few generations ago whose brief dynasty was justifiably overthrown by the worthy Han, Sima Qian's own court. Finally, there is our own lens transforming the First Emperor into the focal point of operas and video games, of films and theme parks. Why we choose to see the First Emperor today as epitomizing martial valour and cultural unity may tell us more about what we desire out of the present rather than the past. All three lenses—the First Emperor's, Sima Qian's and our own—tell us what we want to remember and not necessarily what the Qin story actually was.

The First Emperor of Qin's self-projected image

Had there been no Sima Qian to leave behind his *Shiji* or *Historical Records* that tell us almost everything we know of the First Emperor, how might we have viewed this man based on the physical evidence alone? For example, would we see him and his ancestors as part of mainstream Chinese civilization, or would we see them as western outsiders relative to the dominant cultural sphere of the Zhou Dynasty (1122–256 BCE)? To be blunt, was China's First Emperor Chinese?

If seen through Sima Qian's lens, the people of Qin historically derived their culture from their backward western tribal neighbours; they were 'in the same category as the Rong and Di', a classification clearly intended to be derogatory. Mere backwardness might not have been bothersome to the Central States had Qin quietly remained on the periphery, but the Grand Historiographer lamented that state's greater ambitions because it 'favoured violence and cruelty over benevolence and propriety'.[1] In like manner, its eastern neighbours would complain that Qin 'possessed the mind of a tiger or wolf', failing to recognize ritual or righteousness in its aggressive pursuits.[2] This barbarian and even animal-like stereotype would become embedded within the marketplace of images over the next two millennia. For example, Tang poetry would often romanticize the First Emperor's persona as a fearsome fighter emerging from the pre-imperial Chinese version of the Wild West. As Li Bo (701–762) wrote:

The King of Qin swept through every direction, his tiger gaze so courageous!
Brandishing his sword, he parted the floating clouds, and the feudal lords all came westward.[3]

Both geographically and cosmologically, the tiger symbolized the West throughout imperial history. That is, the First Emperor was not only branded formidable and terrifying, he was also from beyond the cultural milieu of the Central States.

Yet archaeology now tells a different story that would deny Qin's alien status. Housing scores of elaborate bronze vessels, Qin royal tombs since at least the eighth century were by no means humble and backward. Their grave complexes heeded Zhou sumptuary regulations, and their capital cities boasted impressive palaces and temples.

---

[1] *Shiji* (Beijing: Zhonghua shuju, 1985), 15.685. For other similar associations between Qin and its tribal neighbours, see *Shiji*, 5.202 and 68.2234.

[2] *Shiji*, 44.1857.

[3] Yu Xianhao, *Li Bai xuanji* (Shanghai: Shanghai guji, 1990), 461–4 ('Gu feng').

Judging from the physical remains, historical archaeologists argue that the Qin culturally numbered among the Central States throughout much of its history and only in the fourth century BCE pursued a different course after adopting major Legalist reforms that broke up the aristocracy and replaced its power with an increasingly deified ruler. Labels of barbarianism appear in Chinese texts only after this time.[4]

According to another charge levelled against the Qin, this western state was not only barbaric, it was becoming increasingly savage. Sima Qian highlights how Qin in 678 BCE began the practice of burying the living with the dead, and other Han commentators argue such brutality was the natural extension of an earlier tradition of interring human-shaped figurines in the grave.[5] Again archaeology would dismiss these charges. While it is true that the Qin led the other states in substituting imitations for real burial goods, it was not the first step on a slippery slope that led to live burials. Human sacrifice long predated the Qin state and Zhou Dynasty as a whole, and in Qin's time it was no more prevalent there than anywhere else. Relative to this ancient practice of live burials, the earliest known Qin case of human-shaped grave figurines, namely a pair of crudely hewn wooden carvings about 80 cm in height, only dates to around 700 BCE.[6] Excavated in 2006, the oldest known Qin terracotta figurines, specifically a pair of ten-centimetre-tall statuettes found in a ceramics workshop, date back to the beginning of the Warring States Period (481–221).[7] The charge that Qin was becoming increasingly savage as evinced by

[4] Lothar von Falkenhausen, 'Mortuary Behavior in Pre-Imperial Qin: A Religious Interpretation', *Religion and Chinese Society* vol. 1, ed. John Lagerwey (Hong Kong: The Chinese University Press, 2004), 155; Gideon Shelach and Yuri Pines, 'Secondary State Formation and the Development of Local Identity: Change and Continuity in the State of Qin (770–221 BC)', in *Archaeology of Asia*, ed. Miriam T. Stark (Oxford: Blackwell Publishing, 2006), 216.

[5] See *Shiji*, 5.183 and *Mengzi zhengyi* (Beijing: Zhonghua shuju, 1996), 63 ('Liang Hui wang').

[6] Von Falkenhausen, 'Mortuary Behavior in Pre-Imperial Qin: A Religious Interpretation', 129–30.

[7] *People's Daily Online* (15 August 2006), originally reported by the Xinhua News Agency.

its mortuary figurines leading to live burials simply runs contrary to the new archaeological record.

Yet what of the allegation concerning the First Emperor's 'violence and cruelty' exemplified by his martial might? Was the hyperbolic language of Jia Yi (201–169 BCE), quoted in Sima Qian's history, justified when he wrote:

The king of Qin . . . waved his long whip and drove the contents of the cosmos before him, swallowing up the two Zhou [courts] and eliminating the feudal lords. He stepped into the position of highest honour and subdued all in every direction around him; he brandished his staff and club to whip and bastinado all under Heaven, his might causing everywhere within the four seas to quake.[8]

Our modern image of the First Emperor is closely allied with the army of eight thousand life-size terracotta warriors discovered since 1974 near his grave mound in Shaanxi Province. The very nature of that army forces the viewer to shift orders of magnitude, not seeing individual infantrymen or particular archers but a structured military mass. The vast extent of the Emperor's underground terracotta army would seem to justify Jia Yi's awesome image of him, although why the army was created remains a mystery. Was it a dynamic fighting force to fend off his ghostly enemies in the afterlife? Or was it a static definition of his grandeur, an extension of his identity permanently embedded in the silent landscape?

Whatever the answer, archaeology itself is an accidental science, meaning that we can't control what will be discovered or when, although the pace of that science is accelerating. The spate of road, bridge, and factory building in the increasingly industrialized Shaanxi Province has uncovered more than fifty major finds in recent years, including in 2006 a tomb that is thought to belong to the First Emperor's own grandmother.[9] Furthermore while there are no immediate plans to excavate the First Emperor's tomb, archaeologists are indirectly probing its structure with ground penetrating radar, taking electrical resistance measurements and

---

[8] *Shiji*, 6.280.
[9] Petra Kolonko, 'Am Grab der Kaiser-Ahnen', *Frankfurter Allgemeine Zeitung* (1 June 2006), 10.

thousands of core samples, together generating a three-dimensional schematic of the tomb mound's interior. Instead of being pyramid-shaped, the tomb itself is now thought to be like a square volcano with the football-field sized tomb down in the crater and access corridors cutting through the east and west rims.[10] The core samples also reveal high levels of mercury, perhaps confirming Sima Qian's own description of the tomb's micro-cosmos wherein rivers of quicksilver flowed for eternity.[11]

While the tomb interior itself remains the stuff of conjecture, more and more is now known about the pits of grave goods around the tomb, and those pits reveal that the First Emperor's grand martial image, while definitely significant, is only a partial picture. In 1999 excavators within the cemetery complex uncovered a pit containing a dozen life-sized acrobats, their shirtless bodies realistically depicted, with some muscular and heavy-set whereas others were of slighter build. In 2000, they found civil officials wearing long jackets with knives and whetstones hanging from their belts, the knife being a scribe's tool for scraping off wooden and bamboo slats used in record keeping. In 2001, they exhumed from a single tunnel more than two score highly detailed life-sized bronze waterfowl including geese, ducks, and storks, and they uncovered fifteen life-sized terracotta musicians from an adjoining tunnel.[12] When assessing how the First Emperor valued these newly excavated burial goods, we might consider their detail, their material composition, and especially their proximity to the ruler's final resting place. While the terracotta warriors

[10] Marc Grellert, Manfred Koob, and Mieke Pfarr, 'Eine dreidimensionale Computerrekonstruktion der Kaisergräber von Xi'an', in *Xi'an: Kaiserliche Macht im Jenseits* (Mainz: Verlag Philipp von Zabern, 2006), 131–4.

[11] Lion Television in early 2006 aired a two-hour documentary entitled 'The First Emperor: The Man who Made China' on the Discovery Channel that summarizes some of the recent work on the tomb. While it reviewed new evidence about the tomb, this documentary also presented as fact much fanciful speculation, ranging from claims that the First Emperor was an illegitimate child—a claim dating at least to Sima Qian's time—to charges that the First Emperor became a madman who lost his grip on reality in his last years due to mercury poisoning.

[12] For images of these various finds, see Xu Weimin, *Dixia Junchen: Qin Bingma Yong Keng Kaogu Da Faxian* (Hangzhou: Zhejiang wenyi chubanshe, 2002); *War and Peace: Treasures of the Qin and Han Dynasties* (Hong Kong: Hong Kong Museum of History, 2002) and *Xi'an: Kaiserliche Macht im Jenseits*.

are numerous, they still stand a kilometre away from the tomb. The question we might ask ourselves when evaluating the First Emperor's image is how our picture of him based upon the physical evidence alone might have been different had *these* pits been excavated in 1974 rather than those of the infantry and archers.

This cemetery was not necessarily a self-projected image because it was never meant to be exhumed, but the First Emperor did leave behind other physical evidence explicitly intended to vaunt his reputation among the living, namely the mountain inscriptions dedicated to him between 219 and 210 BCE that record his standardization schemes, his compassion for the people, his righteousness, humanity, and wisdom. Set down in the *Historical Records* and translated by Dawson in this selection, they were explicitly inspired by Confucian tradition, and they balance his martial valour with his concern for the people. Instead of the King of Qin merely 'eliminating the feudal lords' in Jia Yi's words, these inscriptions claim that 'Abroad he taught the feudal lords, gloriously bestowing the blessings of culture, and spreading enlightenment by means of the principles of righteousness' (p. 70). They evince that his self-projected image was not intended to be that of a strict, heavily armed Legalist:

Thus he clarifies human affairs, and brings concord to father and son. With sagacity, wisdom, humaneness, and righteousness, he has made manifest all principles . . . . Farming is put first and non-essentials are abolished, and it is the black-headed people who are made wealthy. (pp. 66–7)

While the First Emperor would have chosen to depict himself as a virtuous ruler, the story's principal teller is the Han's Sima Qian, and even though these inscriptions are preserved in the latter's *Historical Records*, each is framed in such a way that we might question the First Emperor's sincerity. That is, Sima Qian faithfully records these Confucian-sounding texts, but between them he describes the First Emperor's search for immortality and his wilder antics. Some modern scholars even speculate that the

stories of his quest for immortality were Sima Qian's later inser-
tions based upon local folklore.[13]

How Sima Qian sees the First Emperor

In 1989 an IMAX documentary entitled 'First Emperor of China'
dramatized the Qin ruler's unification and drew upon the imagery
of the terracotta army. 'Perhaps his empire has lasted for ten
thousand generations after all,' it concluded. 'That would not be
a surprise to Qin, the First Emperor.'[14] In 2006 a documentary
entitled 'The First Emperor' on the Discovery Channel also dramatized the unification and highlighted new finds at the tomb complex, and this documentary carried the subtitle 'The Man who
Made China'.[15] Why didn't Sima Qian share the modern popular
assessment of the First Emperor as a 10,000-generation empire
builder or 'the man who made China'?

Sima Qian was an official of the Han court that had defeated the
fifteen-year Qin Dynasty less than a hundred years earlier, and
that defeat had to be explained. Yet even if the First Emperor had
failed to live up to his own image as a cosmic unifier, he was still
not just another commoner. How might Sima Qian account for the
Emperor's meteoric rise and fall? The Grand Historiographer's
answer was simply that the Qin leaders were in the right place at
the right time, a theme fully developed in the biography of Li Si,
the chief minister of Qin.

Sima Qian preserves an anecdote of Li Si early in his career
observing the rats at his home in Shangcai. The timid rats hid in
the latrine, but the brave rats fearlessly occupied the granary.
Their circumstances shaped their behaviour, and the trick was to
recognize opportunity and take full advantage of it. Sima Qian has
Li Si leaving his teacher with the words, 'I have heard that if one

---

[13] Martin Kern, *The Stele Inscriptions of Ch'in Shih-huang: Text and Ritual in Early Chinese
Imperial Representation* (New Haven, CT: American Oriental Society, 2000), 160.

[14] 'First Emperor of China' (National Film Board of Canada, Canadian Museum of
Civilization and China Xi'an Film Studio, 1989).

[15] 'The First Emperor: The Man who Made China' (Lion Television, 2006) aired on
the Discovery Channel on 29 January 2006.

gets an opportunity one should not be slow to seize it' (p. 23). For him, the right place was the up-and-coming western state of Qin, and the right time was just after the death of its king, leaving a young, malleable heir on the throne—the future First Emperor. He travelled to the Qin court and communicated this same message to the king:

'The ordinary person misses his chances. . . . This is the one opportunity in 10,000 generations. If you are idle and do not press ahead, the feudal states will regain their strength and will combine with each other to form north–south alliances, and even if you had the fine qualities of the Yellow Emperor you would not be able to unify them.' (p. 24)

According to Sima Qian, the young king took this message to heart, grabbed the opportunity, completed the empire and promoted Li Si to its highest office.

The problem with opportunism is that once the opportunist becomes established, other opportunists will find the right time and place to tear down the establishment. When the First Emperor himself dies and leaves the next young, malleable heir on the throne, the dreaded court eunuch Zhao Gao seizes his own chance to help the next ruler, who isn't even the rightful heir but merely a younger, more easily controlled brother. (The rightful heir, Fu Su, was subsequently forced to commit suicide.) Pressuring the younger brother to dragoon the chief minister into their machinations, Zhao Gao exclaims: 'The time has come, the time has come! If we delay, we shall not achieve our plans. There are abundant provisions and swift horses, and the only fear is that we shall be too late' (pp. 31–2). Li Si mistakenly sides with the new political entrepreneur Zhao Gao, but opportunists do not keep friends and Zhao Gao has Li Si executed.

Here Sima Qian may be less historian and more writer as he thoroughly develops his theme. At the end of 'The Annals of Qin' he includes an essay by Jia Yi that addresses the question of why the First Emperor was able to brandish 'his staff and club to whip and bastinado all under Heaven', and his answer is exactly the same as in the Li Si biography. The First Emperor was simply in the right place at the right time. The place was Qin, a state in

Western China that was naturally fortified with surrounding mountains and rivers. From such a citadel, its rulers could descend and crush the other feudal lords. 'Surely it wasn't because [Qin] produced worthies generation after generation?' Jia Yi asks rhetorically. 'It was all because they occupied this vantage point.' Sima Qian himself would modify Jia Yi's thinking, arguing that it wasn't so much the west's mountainous terrain that gave Qin its advantage but something more geomantic. 'The east is where things arise; the west is where things come to fruition,' he explains, and for proof he then lists all of history's great leaders who had first arisen in Western China.[16] Thus Jia Yi and Sima Qian both credited the Qin's location but for different reasons. Topologically or cosmologically, the Qin enjoyed the high ground.

As for being in the right time, the First Emperor found himself at the end of a long period of history without strong kings. As Jia Yi summarized, 'All of the masses longed to secure a peaceful life, and everyone set aside his concerns to put his trust in the sovereign.'[17] The war-weary Central States were dangerously susceptible to anyone who might bring them together, and given this opportunity, the First Emperor only needed to prove himself worthy of the people's adoration. Yet in Jia Yi's opinion, he was too greedy, short-sighted, and self-obsessed, playing the part of a ruler rather than truly becoming one.

By adding Jia Yi's essay to the end of 'The Annals of Qin' and by replicating this message in his Li Si biography and elsewhere, Sima Qian makes the theme of opportunism in his overall Qin story explicit.[18] Yet the very fact that it is a *themed story* should begin to make the careful reader of these translations wary. When does the narrative eclipse the history? When does the storyline dictate selectivity of the facts? When does an anecdote about rats take precedence over the evidence? Here the Grand Historiographer

---

[16] *Shiji*, 15.685–6.

[17] *Shiji*, 6.283.

[18] Dawson's translations do not include the Jia Yi essay. See Burton Watson's translation of *Records of the Grand Historian: Qin Dynasty* (New York: Columbia University Press, 1993), 74–83, or William H. Nienhauser's edition entitled *The Grand Scribe's Records: The Basic Annals of pre-Han China by Ssu-ma Ch'ien* (Bloomington: Indiana University Press, 1994), 163–9.

is really a storyteller; as Dawson rightly points out, Sima Qian is explaining 'traditions' (*zhuan*) about people and not unfolding histories in the modern Western sense. For the Grand Historiographer, the traditions surrounding the First Emperor have all the markings of a tabloid headline:

Sex. The First Emperor's patron, Lü Buwei, hires the well-endowed gigolo Lao Ai to sleep with the future ruler's mother in order to cover up Lü Buwei's own illicit affair with her that led to nothing less than the First Emperor's birth, or so Sima Qian would have us believe. 'Sometimes, to the strains of licentious music, he made Lao Ai...walk along with a wheel of *tong*-wood attached to his penis, and he ensured that the Queen Dowager heard about it so that she might be tempted' (p. 7).

Violence. In a bid for thought control, the First Emperor burned the books that might reveal historical alternatives to his own form of Legalist government, and as for the scholars who were still talking about the Golden Age, 'although they tried to exonerate themselves, more than 460 who had infringed the prohibitions were all buried alive at [the capital] Xianyang, and the whole Empire was made to know about this to serve as a warning for the future' (p. 78).

Mystery. The Emperor was called 'the mysterious one', and no one ever knew in which of his many palaces he was residing. 'And if anyone mentioned the place which he honoured with his presence as he moved about, he would be condemned to death' (p. 76).

Intrigue. After becoming the Chief Minister himself, the eunuch Zhao Gao attempts to drive the second Qin ruler mad and eventually succeeds in forcing him to commit suicide. The third ruler clearly recognized his danger. 'Now supposing I present myself at the ancestral temple after I have fasted, this person intends to kill me, taking advantage of the fact that I am in the temple.' Thus he plotted, 'I will plead illness and not go, and the Chief Minister is bound to come here himself, and when he comes, we will kill him' (p. 93).

And a tear-jerking final scene. As Li Si and one of his sons support each other while walking out to the place of their execution, the former Chief Minister tearfully laments, 'I would like to go with you again and take our tawny dog out through the eastern gate of Shangcai to chase the cunning hare, but how could that be done!' (p. 49).

The cinematic element in these stories should alert us to the possibility of invention.[19]

How we see the First Emperor

Chinese and Japanese plays and films about the First Emperor date back to the 1950s, but his popular image is multifarious. In modern cinema, the closer the film stays to the *Historical Records*, the more negative is the Emperor's image. At this negative end of the spectrum, *The Emperor and the Assassin* (Sony Pictures Classics, 2000) begins and ends with the Emperor being reminded to carry out his ancestors' wishes to unite all under Heaven, although by the end we have learnt to be sceptical because (*a*) we have discovered, along with the First Emperor, that he is really the bastard son of Lü Buwei from Zhao and not descended from Qin rulers and (*b*) just before the credits roll, we are reminded that Qin unity collapsed within fifteen years. More importantly, the Qin sovereign began the film as a well-intentioned unifier, but by the final curtain he is simply a tyrant as bad as any other.

At the other end of the spectrum are films such as *Hero* (Miramax, 2002) that have little to do with Sima Qian's history. An assassin named Broken Sword has realized through his study of calligraphy that if something is to endure it must return to a state of simplicity, and he understands that, in terms of the Central States, simplicity equates with unity. To dissuade one of his cohorts from killing the Qin unifier, he instructs this second assassin by writing in the sand the two characters 'all under Heaven' (*tianxia*), a phrase denoting territorial totality since the earliest Confucian and Daoist classics. After this second assassin

---

[19] For six examples of questionable interpolations in the *Historical Records*, see Derk Bodde, 'The State and Empire of Ch'in', *The Cambridge History of China* vol. 1, eds. Denis Twitchett and Michael Loewe (Cambridge: Cambridge University Press, 1986), 94–8.

relates Broken Sword's lesson to the Emperor himself, the Emperor exclaims:

'Who would have thought an assassin would understand me the best! Alone in my position, I have endured endless criticism, endless attempts on my life. No one has ever grasped what I have been trying to do. Even my own court regards me as a tyrant. And yet, Broken Sword, a man I barely knew, was able to see clearly what is truly in my heart.'

This unity-espousing emperor bears little resemblance to that portrayed in *The Emperor and the Assassin* or indeed in Sima Qian's *Historical Records*.

Sitting somewhere between these two ends of the spectrum are films such as *The Emperor's Shadow* (Fox Lorber Films, 1999) that very loosely draw upon a handful of stories found in Sima Qian such as that of the musician Gao Jianli. Here the main metaphor is music, and Gao looks forward to all musical notes becoming standardized as a result of unification. Furthermore, the different musical qualities of each state will become harmonized with one another as the Qin martial drums find common voice with the fine zither music of Yan. Portrayed as an aesthete, the Emperor ultimately wants a single imperial anthem because, along with unifying the currency, weights, measures, and language, he also wants to unify the minds of his people. Yet the film ends with Gao's own failed assassination attempt, and just before he dies on the palace steps the would-be killer predicts, 'History will record that when you were installed I attacked you', to which the Emperor responds, 'Wrong: I write the history books, and they will say I kept you alive because you are my eternal shadow.' The audience well knows that Sima Qian preserved the story of Gao Jianli's attempted assassination and that it is in fact the Emperor who is wrong. We are explicitly not seeing the Emperor's self-projected image but instead looking through Sima Qian's lens.

Representations of 'The Man who Made China' are by no means limited to the silver screen. Asia Television Limited (Hong Kong) dramatized the First Emperor's life over the course of roughly fifty television episodes. Books range from the generally factual account of Jonathan Clement's *The First Emperor of China* to the bizarre speculations of Maurice Cotterell's *The Terracotta Warriors: The Secret Codes of the Emperor's Army* in which the warriors' hair skeins mimic the sun's magnetic field, their varied hand positions reveal secret numerical codes, and the Braille-like rivets on their armour contain hidden messages.[20] One fictional work identifies the First Emperor as an alien exile stranded on earth, and another transforms his terracotta warriors into an army of robots. In computer games one can explore the Emperor's tomb in the adventure-puzzle game 'Qin: Tomb of the Middle Kingdom',[21] or one can build a global empire in his name via the strategy game 'Sid Meier's "Civilization IV"'.[22] Even the Emperor's rightful heir, Fu Su, becomes the protagonist in the action role-playing game 'Prince of Qin'.[23] Here instead of committing suicide, Fu Su ventures off to the capital to face down Zhao Gao and various possessed terracotta enemies. On the stage, in 2006 the New York Metropolitan Opera cast Plácido Domingo in the role of Tan Dun's *The First Emperor* in an extremely elaborate remake of *The Emperor's Shadow*. Amidst the proposals to build a theme park beside his tomb and the ubiquitous image of his netherworld army now even appearing on Coca-Cola bottles, the First Emperor has achieved an unforeseen kind of immortality in the twenty-first century that ranges from the glitzy to the glamorous.

What is it about the First Emperor that has earned him this immortality today despite Sima Qian's dismissal of him as an opportunist? Obviously his martial valour attracts film-goers, gamers, and adventure-loving readers, but another attraction is that he is only one man, a single individual rising above a distant, complex, and confused history of warring states. Chinese unification

---

[20] Jonathan Clements, *The First Emperor of China* (Phoenix Mill, England: Sutton Publishing, 2006); Maurice Cotterell, *The Terracotta Warriors: The Secret Codes of the Emperor's Army* (Rochester, VT: Bear & Company, 2004).

[21] 'Qin: Tomb of the Middle Kingdom' (SouthPeak Interactive, 1995).

[22] 'Sid Meier's "Civilization IV"' (Firaxis Games, 2005). The author of this Preface is proud to report that, in his role as First Emperor, he won the space race but sadly had to wipe out the British, Roman, and Aztec empires in the process.

[23] 'Prince of Qin' (Strategy First, 2002). The author of this Preface regrets to report that, in his role as Fu Su, he never made it very far south of the Great Wall before he was eaten by a 'tiger-fish'.

is reduced to a single emperor; the entire Qin Dynasty centres on a single person. If Sima Qian is to be believed, the First Emperor himself is responsible for cultivating this image of aloof soloist. He records one complaint against him thus: 'The business of the Empire, no matter whether trivial or important, is all decided by the Supreme One, who goes so far as to have the documents weighed, so that he cannot rest until he has dealt with the right number of documents for that day and night' (p. 77). In like manner the Emperor broke with tradition by choosing not to establish his relatives to oversee the more distant kingdoms on his behalf and instead funnelled all power through himself. Just as his empire became unified into one state, he himself became explicitly singular, and so evolved into an easily preserved symbol within the communal memory.

Thus the First Emperor as a symbol of unity possessed the potential to survive; but why is he enjoying particular popularity in the twenty-first century? First, Chinese economic development can be directly linked with a general upsurge in historical awareness. A higher standard of living allows more opportunity to explore one's cultural foundations.[24] This development not only fuels interest in the past, it literally uncovers more of that past as road, dam, and factory construction reveals more and more archaeological sites. Yet the speed of this development should not be overemphasized. In 2006, it still cost a tenth of a person's average monthly income in Shaanxi just to visit the terracotta warriors.[25] Second, the particular popularity of the First Emperor is perhaps related to an even grander form of perceived unity developing in the present century. Once also considered an outsider by the dominant cultural sphere to its east, China is conscious of its growing leadership role in an increasingly interdependent world stage. It remains to be seen whether the global village's oldest, largest, and fastest developing resident will soon become its mayor. 'All under Heaven' now means '*all* under Heaven'.

[24] Kishore Mahbubani, *Can Asians Think? Understanding the Divide between East and West* (South Royalton, VT: Steerforth Press, 2002), 26–7.
[25] Kolonko, 'Am Grab der Kaiser-Ahnen', 10.

INTRODUCTION

Historical Records (*Shiji*) is the most famous Chinese historical work, which not only established a pattern for later Chinese historical writing, but was also much admired for its literary qualities, not only in China, but also in Japan, where it became available as early as the eighth century AD.

What makes it particularly remarkable to the modern eye is the complexity of its construction. It is not a mere narrative history. There are five sections: first come the basic annals, then the chronological tables, then treatises concerning the history of matters considered to be of importance to the state, then histories of states which existed prior to the unification of China, and finally a section which is largely biographical. The whole massive work, in 130 chapters, is meant to contain a history of the Chinese world from the beginning down to about 100 BC, the time when it was being written.

The size of the work, together with its complicated structure, present a difficulty for anyone wishing to provide a sample for readers of Oxford World's Classics. Consequently I have decided to restrict this selection to material relevant to the Qin Dynasty and its founder. This has several advantages: the dynasty was short-lived, lasting less than two decades altogether; it was the dynasty that unified China in 221 BC and founded the Empire that, despite long periods of division and of domination by alien peoples, was to survive until its replacement by a republic after the revolution of 1911. Happily too, it is a period that is less unfamiliar than some to English-speaking readers, especially since it was founded by the emperor known to history as Qin Shi Huangdi (First Emperor of Qin), whose tomb near Xi'an was guarded by the so-called 'terracotta warriors' which were unearthed in 1974 and are now one of China's main tourist attractions.

The word Qin is perhaps better known to many readers in the romanization 'Ch'in', which was widely current until recent times. It is thought to have been the word that lay behind the modern names for that part of the world such as 'China' and 'la Chine', while the term 'Sinology', meaning Chinese studies, must also have derived from the same origin. But although the Qin Dynasty was responsible for unifying China and laying the foundations of empire, the Chinese people have not looked back on this age with pride, and so have not adopted it for the name of their country, which has throughout the imperial period, and indeed since, been known as 'the Middle Kingdom'. Indeed, when they have wished to adopt for themselves names derived from dynastic periods, they have fastened on revered dynasties like Han and Tang, and sometimes referred to themselves as 'men of Han' or 'men of Tang'.

The reason for their unwillingness to call themselves men of Qin is plain enough. The Qin were notorious for several episodes which made them synonymous with tyranny in the eyes of their successors. The unification of China was a task that could be achieved only by the deployment of extreme ruthlessness. One event that has stood out among all others as the target of vilification is the so-called 'burning of the books' in 213 BC. The purpose of this destruction of literature was to monopolize learning for the benefit of the court by causing sensitive material to be available only to the seventy court academicians (or, more literally, scholars of broad learning), leaving only works of practical value at the disposal of a wider readership. This was the most notorious of the literary inquisitions that have disfigured Chinese history, and it was made more serious by the conflagration at the end of this short-lived dynasty, for it seems to have destroyed much of what had survived in the imperial library. We are, of course, not in a position to know how effective this measure was (although much was made of the attempts to rediscover and reconstitute ancient works in the succeeding Han Dynasty), but the episode obviously provided rich material for anti-Qin propagandists in later decades and centuries, so that ultimately Qin darkness and barbarism came to be directly contrasted with Confucian light and civilization.

A second enterprise with which the name of Qin is indissolubly associated is the building of the Great Wall. So much had been achieved during the First Emperor's reign, since all the great powers had fallen to his armies in the last decade prior to unification, that the supreme task of his period as emperor was clearly to consolidate these gains. Although he might claim that the Qin Dynasty would last for 10,000 reigns, he had to do as much as he could to preserve his conquests. It is a cliché that the Great Wall is the only man-made object that can be seen from the moon. It is also one of the main tourist sights of contemporary China, and all kinds of distinguished visitors have been filmed thereon by the world's television cameras. But what is to be seen nowadays near Beijing is the reconstruction made during the Ming Dynasty (1368–1644), which succeeded the Yuan Dynasty of the alien Mongols and was deeply concerned to put up barriers against any resurgence of Mongol power.

The actual extent of the original Qin building operations is far from clear. The northern states had already erected defensive barriers on their frontiers to keep out the barbarians, and the Qin were driven by the relentless logic of the situation to link these up and try to form a material demarcation between the sedentary Chinese, who were dependent on the raising of crops, and the nomadic non-Chinese people of the north, who were prone to find easy pickings by raiding the fat lands to their south. The logistics of wall-building over such terrain are frightening, so it is not surprising that vast numbers of convict-labourers were employed upon this task and that the death rate was extremely high. At the same time a force of 700,000 convict-labourers was being employed on the construction of the imperial tomb; and the discovery of the 'terracotta warriors', more than 7,000 individually represented soldiers, together with their horses and chariots—part of the force deployed to defend the magnificent tomb, whose description in the *Historical Records* still awaits verification—lends credence to the idea that a vast amount of resources and skill was invested in this endeavour. At any rate, to the resentment of the intellectuals at the burning of the books was added the resentment of the labouring masses at the enormous physical burdens placed upon the people by such great construction enterprises as the Great Wall and the imperial tomb.

Another category of people who suffered hugely from the Qin success was the leading families of the various independent states that had until recently comprised China. If the records are to be

believed 200,000 of these people were removed from their localities
and housed near the capital, presumably together with their families and household servants, so that the Qin could keep a close eye
on them.

So, lasting as it did for less than two decades, the Qin left behind
a legacy that was bound to receive extremely hostile attention
in the writings of future historians. The Qin's place in history is
reminiscent of that of the short-lived Sui Dynasty, which
reunified China before the glorious Tang took over early in the
seventh century AD. Although the Sui emperors had appreciated
the propaganda value of utilizing the support of all the main
schools of thought, Confucianism, Daoism, and Buddhism, they
nevertheless suffered from a similar urge to get things done in too
much of a hurry and their tyrannical methods could be made
much of by Confucian historians now fully imbued with the doctrine of the bad last ruler who had forfeited the Mandate of
Heaven as a result of his wickedness, while writers of popular
fiction could regale their readers with bizarre reports of the sexual
prowess and inclinations of the Emperor Yang, who was said to
have progressed down the newly constructed canals in an ornate
barge pulled by his concubines, and to have had a great city built
to house his harem rather than for geopolitical reasons.

It is plain therefore that the Qin Dynasty has suffered from a
bad press throughout most of Chinese history, although there was
a brief period during the Great Proletarian Cultural Revolution
when, in association with the anti-Confucius campaign, the more
positive aspects of the Qin achievement were emphasized. Is it then
possible to get at the reality behind the propaganda? Apart from the
major tyrannical enterprises which have just been mentioned—
the construction of the tomb, the building of the Great Wall, and
the settling of huge numbers of potential dissidents in the environs of the capital—the sources assume that the evil of Qin was
very much due to its being a Legalist regime.

The Legalist philosophy had its origin in Qin under the aus-
pices of Lord Shang, a minister originally from the state of Wey
whose doctrines are allegedly set out in the *Book of Lord Shang*,
the first of two major Legalist works. The philosophy contained

in this book lays much stress on the kind of militaristic values that one might expect an ambitious dictator to hold. It also stresses agriculture as compared to other economic activities. There is emphasis on the doctrine of mutual responsibility to ensure that families and communities police themselves for fear that all would suffer punishment for any crime committed by a member of the group. Ethical and old-fashioned cultural values are attacked, and the relentless rule of law is meant to prevail over Confucian casuistry and family values.

But it is important to realize that the slate was not wiped clean of earlier tradition. Obviously, Legalist ideas did have an impact and did assist the Qin in the ruthless and efficient pursuit of their goals, but it is not in the nature of human affairs for the past to be completely wiped out. Even in a modern society, with all the tools of propaganda at its disposal and a relentless desire to change the very nature of human motivation, it is amazing how resilient old-fashioned beliefs and practices can be; so that with a slight relaxation in contemporary China out from the cupboard came the ancestral tablets and joss-sticks burnt again in the temples. The Qin Dynasty lasted for such a short time that the philosophy of Legalism cannot have had as profound an impact as is sometimes assumed.

A reading of the *Historical Records* does reveal some Legalist influence, but at the same time it is interesting how the Legalist message, even in the mouth of someone like Zhao Gao, the eunuch who was the power behind the throne at the end of the dynasty, is depicted as following the time-honoured practice of quoting from ancient literary sources and models from antiquity. The author of the *Historical Records* was naturally incapable of depicting dyed-in-the-wool Legalist villains, however much Legalism may have been blamed for Qin villainy. One is struck, too, by the wording of the inscriptions on tablets erected throughout the Empire as the First Emperor went on his travels. As may be seen from a reading of 'The Annals of Qin' (Chapter 5) these are full of the grandiose language one would expect from the scribes of a supreme monarch traversing his vast new empire, and the Legalist influence is not very conspicuous.

Of course, it must be recognized that the *Historical Records* is not concerned with the business of history-writing as we know it today. It has much to do with the outline of political and military events and the deeds of great men, and little to do with grand modern conceptions like causation. To get a clearer idea of what life was like at the grass roots one needs more information from the vast treasure trove of archaeological discovery which has emerged under the People's Republic of China. For example, in 1975 a handbook of Qin law was discovered in the grave of an official who in 235 BC was charged with the business of trying criminal cases. Although the law described was clearly operative in the state of Qin some years before the unification and establishment of the Empire in 221 BC, it is reasonable to assume that much of it would have been put into use under the Qin Dynasty. Two points are particularly striking: one is the great detail and sophistication of the legal procedures, and the other is that the system described, although harsh by present-day European standards, does not portray Qin society as distinctively so in comparison with other Chinese societies of antiquity. In fact, from some points of view the Qin may be seen as a stage in the increasing centralization and bureaucratization of China, exposed to vilification because it trod on many toes in its rush to create something lasting and inevitable. It should also be remembered that, although scholars nowadays tend to think that sophisticated systems of law were in earlier and wider operation than was at once thought, Confucian anti-Legalism has tended to mask this fact.

In order to set the Qin Dynasty in its historical context it is necessary to look at ancient Chinese history through a wider-angled lens. The preceding dynasty, the Zhou, had been established at some time during the eleventh century BC, with its chief city in the area of Xianyang (present-day Xi'an), where the Qin Dynasty was eventually to have its capital. It seems to have exercised hegemony over a loose confederation of northern Chinese states which had assisted in overcoming the previous dynasty, the Yin (or Shang). The extent and strength of its control was traditionally emphasized in China and its sphere of influence was even supposed to have included the state of Chu in the Yangtze valley, which in fact had a very different culture and for a long time was the chief enemy as far as the northern Chinese states were concerned. Modern scholars have various opinions as to the extent of Zhou control and influence, but what is quite clear is that before long the subordinate states began to demonstrate their independence from Zhou and to absorb their smaller neighbours. In the seventh century BC there was a league of northern Chinese states, which was first of all under the hegemony of the state of Qi in the north-east and secondly under the hegemony of Jin, which was situated in the great bend of the Yellow River where the modern province of Shanxi is to be found. The ostensible purpose of this league was to support the now small and enfeebled Zhou regime, but in reality the confederates were concerned to settle disputes among their members and offer united opposition to the growing power of Chu in the south.

By this time the Zhou capital had had to be moved to the area of present-day Luoyang; and it is also during the seventh century BC that the state of Qin first came to prominence on the Chinese stage. Being far away from the ancient centres of Confucianism in Lu and Qi in north-eastern China and having later spawned the hated Legalist philosophy, it tended to have a semi-barbarian image in ancient China, but it did occupy territory which had constituted the heartlands of the original Zhou regime. At the same time it is assumed that the Qin regime was militarily hardened by its proximity to the barbarian people of Ba and Shu in present-day Sichuan, which it eventually seized from Chu in the late fourth century BC.

For the last one and a half centuries of the so-called Zhou Dynasty China went through what is termed the Warring States period, a time of conflict between the handful of major states which had survived from the internecine struggles of the preceding centuries. The rulers of these states began to usurp the title of king (*wang*), which had belonged, for example, to Kings Wen and Wu, who had laid the foundations for the revered Zhou Dynasty. Philosophical writings revealed a nostalgia for the golden age of the early Zhou Dynasty and a feeling that society was waiting for a restoration of rule over 'all under Heaven'. It was argued that the world would flock to any ruler who governed his state benevolently. But it was of course the force of arms which brought victory and, despite attempts to forge alliances that would thwart the menace of Qin, in fact the major states fell one after another in quick succession, the six most powerful all being conquered in the decade before the final unification. The destruction of the Zhou reigning house had in fact already taken place in 256 BC, but by this time its obliteration was of symbolical rather than practical significance.

Although the political changes dating from the period preceding the Qin Dynasty can easily be outlined, it is not so easy to document changes in the fabric of Chinese society. It is clear that new methods of centralized administration had developed as the states grew larger, particularly stimulated by the need to administer conquered territories. Social change inevitably followed these changes in political organization, with aristocratic predominance gradually giving way to the kind of meritocratic tendency that was to be the norm in imperial China. It is obvious too that technological changes had fostered a development in warfare from the old-fashioned system in which chariot-borne aristocrats were at the centre of events to what was more like mass warfare using iron rather than bronze weapons. Plainly also there had been a gradual development from a barter economy to a money economy, land was being bought and sold, and, despite Confucian contempt for the merchant class, these people were increasingly beginning to wield power.

In fact the merchant Lü Buwei even became Chief Minister of Qin in the year 250 BC, a most extraordinary achievement for someone who had made his fortune in this way: such a success was never surpassed in later centuries by people of this class. What can less confidently be put down to his credit is the claim that he was the natural father of the First Emperor of Qin, who was born in 259 BC and came to the throne of Qin in 246 BC, reigning as king over the state until he unified China twenty-five years later. This story found its way into the *Historical Records* along with other improbable anecdotal material which infiltrated into the account either through the unsurprising gullibility of its author or through insertion by later malicious hands. When he reached adulthood in 238 BC he began to wield power, but in 210 BC, while still only in his fiftieth year, he died suddenly while on tour. In the circumstances no true account of his life survives; instead we have a collection of stories of the kind one would expect to be associated with tyrants.

Sima Qian, the author of the *Historical Records*, took an exuberant interest in good stories and would certainly not have felt the need to submit his material to the kind of scrutiny that would have worried the conscience of a modern historian. The ancient Chinese historical style was in any case to preserve traditions rather than to get at the truth. Sima Qian's object was, as he said himself, to place on record the achievements of great men. It is to be seen in the context of a society in which filial piety was of great importance, and one of the supreme duties of filial piety was to conduct oneself in such a way that an account of one's deeds would be handed down to later generations and thus bring credit to one's ancestors.

In talking about the Chinese historical tradition one has to be very careful to qualify this term. The development of a distinct body of literature separately recognized as history was only a very gradual process. The pre-Qin writings which we categorize as history consisted of works that had a very different aim from that of the modern historian. In remote antiquity rulers needed to have in their entourage people who could place on record and preserve oracular responses concerning important state events and people who were expert at elucidating the links between natural phenomena and human events. It is clear too that at an early stage the text of interstate agreements would have had to be placed on record. The recording of all these kinds of material would inevitably have led to the production of crude annals. One of the most puzzling phenomena in the study of ancient China is the fact that Confucius's greatest claim to fame was his edition of the annals of his native state of Lu. The theory was that the wording of this dry chronicle was so adjusted as to secretly confer praise or blame on the participants in historical events, but a careful analysis of the contents rules out the possibility of such an interpretation.

Various 'traditions' explained the wording of the Lu annals, and three of these have survived. One of them, the *Zuo Tradition*, was mixed up at an early stage with a narrative account of the history of the northern states. Again this latter work could not be described as history in anything like the modern sense, but rather as a collection of anecdotes, and it has as much to do with the origins of literature in story-telling as with the origins of history. There is also an ancient work called the *Shu Jing*, or *Book of Documents*, which in the Han period became one of the hallowed Classics, but it is a work of uncertain date with later accretions constituting about half the book as it now exists. It purports to consist of material such as speeches made by ancient rulers and their ministers and is in the nature of historical source material rather than history. At the same time it should be remembered that anecdotes about ancient rulers and ministers often provided material to support the arguments of those whom we have tended to classify as philosophers.

Sima Qian did not see himself as heir to a distinctive history-writing tradition. His final chapter is autobiographical and tells how he came to write the *Historical Records*. It was his father, Sima Tan, who had conceived the idea and who, in a moving deathbed scene, urged his son to complete the work. Sima Tan looked upon it as the hereditary task of the family to produce such a compilation since they had been Grand Astrologers even in ancient times. By now the task had expanded from the compilation of a dry annalistic account to the story of the Chinese world from the beginning right down to their own times in the reign of the famous Emperor Wu of the Former Han Dynasty. The word *shi*, as an analysis of the Yin Dynasty character indicates, apparently used to refer to the official whose task was to record hits in archery contests and later developed responsibility for the recording of astronomical events, the results of divination, and other matters of importance to the rulers of states. Eventually it began to merit the translation of 'historian', a construction which it has continued to bear down to the present day. I have therefore followed the tradition in referring to the book compiled by Sima Qian as the *Historical Records* as well as the practice of referring to the author as the Grand Historiographer where appropriate in the translation, although it has to be remembered that the title would not have merited such a translation when held by the Sima's ancestors in the Zhou Dynasty. It must also be appreciated that both Sima Qian and his father were not officially employed as historians, as came to be the case with those who were employed by the state to compile dynastic histories.

As I have said, Sima Qian did not see himself as the heir to a tradition of history-writing in anything like a modern sense of the term. Rather he saw himself as a preserver of tradition about great men, as his autobiographical chapter shows. Given the lack of precedent, the most extraordinary thing about the *Historical Records* is its structure. Sima Qian did not content himself with a mere narrative history. He had an understanding of the complexities of history-writing. He divided the work into five sections. First of all there were the basic annals, and indeed our translation includes the main part of chapter 6, which consists of the Basic Annals of the First Emperor of Qin. Secondly there were the chronological tables which skilfully assembled and set out the important political events of the period covered by the book. Thirdly came the treatises, the purpose of which was to deal in turn with the history of some of the matters of particular importance in the eyes of the Government, such as the calendar, the waterways, state religious practices, and so on. Unfortunately this section of the book is clearly in a less complete form than the rest of the work, but it sets a valuable example followed by the writers of the later dynastic histories. Fourthly comes the section known as the Hereditary Houses, which mainly deals with the history of the feudal states that existed before the Qin unified China, and finally comes a section entitled *lie zhuan*—using the same word *zhuan* as is employed in the *Zuozhuan*, or *Zuo Tradition*—meaning 'arranged traditions'. The content of this last but longest section is mainly biographies of famous men of the ages concerned, but it also includes collective biographies (as, for example, those that deal with the 'harsh officials' or the 'wandering knights') together with accounts of the history of foreign peoples with whom the Chinese came into contact.

The second great achievement of the *Historical Records* is the vividness of the writing. It must be remembered that, although he apparently felt that it was his duty in filling his hereditary post to compile such a work, Sima Qian was not under any obligation to do so. It is difficult to decide exactly how much material he obtained from written sources, but clearly much of the liveliness must have come from the strong oral traditions of the day. In adapting the archaic language of the *Zuo Tradition* for some of his chapters in the Hereditary Houses section he showed great skill in making the material accessible to contemporary audiences, but in the final section his love of a good story is given free rein, and at the same time he sees and demonstrates with his final summing-up on each person that the 'innumerable biographies' of which he can only give a sample is the essence of history.

With his sophisticated approach to the writing of history in separate sections, Sima Qian set a pattern which was followed in the dynastic histories, but these were compiled by bureaucrats as reference works for the use of other bureaucrats so they were bound to lack the vividness of Sima Qian's composition. On the other hand, in order to do justice to the great tradition of Chinese historiography, it must be pointed out that total sterility did not set in and there were many other interesting and original developments. However, in order to attempt to provide the non-specialist reader with an illustration of this seminal work I have, as I indicated earlier, provided some translations of chapters which are concerned with the Qin Dynasty and its founder.

But before I do so I shall attempt to assist an understanding of why Sima Qian embarked on this great work by providing an extract from the autobiographical postface to the *Historical Records*. This chapter starts with an account of the history of the Sima family going back to remote antiquity and has little about Sima's father, Sima Tan, except the complete text of a discussion from his pen on the important points of the Six Schools (the Yin-Yang school, the Confucians, the Mohists, the School of Names, the Legalists, and the Daoists). Then it goes on as follows:

Since the Grand Historiographer had been in charge of astronomy, he did not administer the people. He had a son called Qian. Qian was born at Longmen. He ploughed and kept flocks on the sunny slopes of the mountains near the Yellow River. By the age of 10 he was reading aloud the ancient writings. At twenty he journeyed south to the Yangtze and Huai Rivers, ascended Kuaiji to search for the cave of Yu, espied Jiuyi, went by water down to Yun and Xiang, journeyed north and crossed the Wen and Si to investigate the traditions in the cities of Qi and Lu, and observed the customs handed down by Master Kong, and took part in the archery competition held at Mount Yi in Cou. He suffered distress in Po, Xie, and Pengcheng, and returned home via Liang and Chu. Afterwards Qian served as a palace gentleman, and received orders to be sent on the western expedition to the south of Ba and Shu. Having gone south and captured Qiong, Ze, and Kunming, they returned and made their report on the mission.

In that year the Son of Heaven inaugurated the *feng* sacrifice of the Han house, but the Grand Historiographer was left behind at Zhounan and could not join in the activities. Consequently he became so exasperated that he was about to die. It so happened that his son Qian was returning from the mission and saw his father somewhere between the Yellow and Luo Rivers. The Grand Historiographer grasped Qian's hand. 'Our forebears were Grand Historians of the Zhou house,' he said with tears in his eyes. 'From highest antiquity they achieved distinction and honour in the times of Shun and the Xia Dynasty, being in charge of astronomical matters. In later generations they went into decline, and will the chain be severed by me? When you in your turn become Grand Historian, you will carry on from our ancestors. At this moment the Son of Heaven, receiving a thread which has been handed on for 1,000 years, is performing the *feng* sacrifice at Mount Tai, and I cannot go along too. This is my fate, is it not! When I die, you are bound to become the Grand Historian; and having become Grand Historian, do not forget what I intended to argue and put down in writing. Moreover filial piety starts in the service of parents, is next to be found in the service of rulers, and finally in the establishment of one's own character. For the most important aspect of filial piety is for your name to be spread abroad in later generations in order to bring glory to your father and mother. Now all under Heaven sang the praises of the Duke of Zhou, saying that he was able to discuss and sing the virtues of Wen and Wu, proclaim the odes of Zhou and Shao, make known the thoughts of King Tai and Wang Ji, going as far back as Gong Liu, so as to pay honour to Hou Ji.

'After Yu and Lei the kingly ways became defective and the rites and music declined, but Master Kong repaired the old and restored what had been discarded, and when he discussed the *Songs* and *Documents* and created the *Spring* and *Autumn,* men of learning right down to the present have taken him as their model. Since the capture of the unicorn more than 400 years have elapsed and, since some of the states have annexed others, historical records have been abandoned and cut off. Now the Han has risen up and all within the seas is united and, although I became Grand Historian, I have not discussed and placed on record the enlightened sovereigns, talented rulers, loyal ministers and public servants who would die from a sense of duty. I am extremely fearful that the historical writings of all under Heaven will be discarded, and you should really let your thoughts dwell on this!' 'Although your young son is not intelligent,' said Qian, bowing his head and weeping, 'he begs to discuss everything which our forebears have reported concerning ancient times. He will not dare to leave any gaps in it.'

A little later in this autobiographical postface we find the following:

The Grand Historiographer remarked: 'My father had a saying: "Five hundred years from the death of the Duke of Zhou there was Master Kong. From the death of Master Kong right up to now it is 500 years. There is the ability to persevere with the work of the far-sighted generations, to rectify the tradition of the *Book of Changes,* to continue the *Spring and Autumn,* to base oneself on a world defined by the *Songs, Documents, Rites* and *Music.*" His thoughts were set upon these things! His thoughts were set upon these things! How dare his son draw back from them?'

So we are lucky enough to possess Sima Qian's own words, explaining his reason for undertaking this mammoth task. He was much moved by the desire to perpetuate the glories of the past, and he also accepted his father's vision that the Simas were in the Mencian tradition that a sage was due every 500 years, the time which had elapsed since Confucius's day. More than 2,000 years after his death his vision and determination still shine through.

NOTE ON THE TEXT

ACCORDING to the autobiographical postface of the *Historical Records* the work consisted of 526,500 characters, and one copy was placed by its author in the capital and another apparently in a hiding-place outside the capital in case disaster should befall, as indeed had happened once before when historical documents stored in the imperial library had been obliterated by the conflagration at the end of the Qin. In the *History of the Former Han Dynasty* we are also told that a grandson of Sima Qian publicized the book, so that it was consulted widely. Unfortunately, however, parts of the work were incomplete and additions were made by another hand. Moreover, parts of the present text are closely similar to the relevant portions of the *History of the Former Han Dynasty*, so that it is not clear which was copied from which. Some passages may have been maliciously inserted, but the motivation for depicting the First Emperor in an unfavourable light belonged to Sima Qian as much as anyone, especially in view of the indignities he suffered under a later tyrant.

It soon became necessary to elucidate difficulties in the text, so that the powerful Chinese tradition of commentary operated on the *Historical Records* almost throughout its existence. This tradition has survived under the People's Republic, and for this translation I have used mainly the most accessible modern edition, which was published by the Zhonghua Shuju in 1959.

There are many possible attitudes to translation, but my own method has been to try to get as close as possible to the original, even at the risk of inelegance. It would of course be possible to make Sima Qian sound as if he were writing in the late twentieth century, but it seems to me that more might be lost than gained. The language may occasionally appear too honorific or humilific for contemporary tastes, but I have preferred to render it as accurately as possible, although the words may sometimes be as empty

as the 'dear sirs' and 'yours faithfullys' of epistolary English. I have,
however, made one concession to the non-specialist reader: as in
my version of the *Analects* (Oxford World's Classics, 1993) I have
occasionally adapted the personal names.

SELECT BIBLIOGRAPHY

THE scholar who has done most to bring the writings of Sima Qian to the English reader is Burton Watson, who in 1961 published two volumes of translations, one devoted to the early years of the Han Dynasty and the other to the age of Emperor Wu of the Han. More than thirty years later, at the end of 1992, it was announced that the publication of a third volume, on the Qin Dynasty, was imminent, and at the same time the two original volumes were to be reissued in Pinyin romanization. These have now been published under the title *Records of the Grand Historian, by Sima Qian* (Hong Kong, 1993).

Although such a coincidence was unfortunate in a field where there are so few workers, the overlap between our books is less than it might have been, partly because much relevant material already comes in Watson's earlier volumes, and partly because he has included much more material from the period before Qin was able to unify China. Those who wish to know more about the historian's life should read Watson's *Ssu ma Ch'ien: Grand Historian of China* (New York, 1958).

On the historical background it is sufficient to refer to the first volume of *The Cambridge History of China*, which is entitled *The Ch'in and Han Empires, 221 BC to AD 220* (Cambridge, 1986). This has rich bibliographical information for anyone who wishes to explore further. A well-illustrated account of a visit to the tomb, with chapters on the historical context, is Arthur Cotterell's *The First Emperor of China: The Story behind the Terracotta Army of Mount Li* (Harmondsworth, 1981).

A collection of articles which will give the reader some idea of the range of history-writing in the Far East is W. G. Beasley and E. G. Pulleyblank (eds.), *Historians of China and Japan* (London, 1961).

Editions of the Historical Records

The Grand Scribe's Records in nine volumes, ed. William H. Nienhauser, Jr. (Bloomington, In. 1994–in progress).

Critical studies on the development of the Qin state

The Cambridge History of Ancient China: From the Origins of Civilization to 221 BC, eds. Michael Loewe and Edward L. Shaughnessy (Cambridge, 1999).

Lothar von Falkenhausen, 'Mortuary Behavior in Pre-Imperial Qin: A Religious Interpretation', *Religion and Chinese Society* vol. 1, ed. John Lagerwey (Hong Kong, 2004), 109–72.

Martin Kern, *The Stele Inscriptions of Ch'in Shih-huang: Text and Ritual in Early Chinese Imperial Representation* (New Haven, Ct, 2000).

Gideon Shelach and Yuri Pines, 'Secondary State Formation and the Development of Local Identity: Change and Continuity in the State of Qin (770–221 BC)', in *Archaeology of Asia*, ed. Miriam T. Stark (Oxford, 2006), 202–30.

Critical studies and aids to reading the Historical Records

Stephen W. Durrant, *The Cloudy Mirror: Tension and Conflict in the Writings of Sima Qian* (Albany, NY, 1995).

Grant Hardy, *Worlds of Bronze and Bamboo: Sima Qian's Conquest of History* (New York, 1999).

Mark Edward Lewis, *Writing and Authority in Early China* (Albany, NY, 1999).

Michael Loewe, *A Biographical Dictionary of the Qin, Former Han & Xin Periods (221 BC–AD 24)* (Leiden, 2000).

Michael Nylan, 'Sima Qian: A True Historian?', *Early China* 23–24 (1998–1999), 203–46.

Recent exhibitions on the First Emperor's mausoleum

First Emperor, ed. Jane Portal (British Museum Press, 2007).

War and Peace: Treasures of the Qin and Han Dynasties (Hong Kong, 2002).

Xi'an: Kaiserliche Macht im Jenseits—Grabfunde und Tempelschätze aus Chinas alter Hauptstadt (Mainz, 2006).

Popular biography on the First Emperor

Jonathan Clements, *The First Emperor of China* (Phoenix Mill, England, 2006).

CHRONOLOGY

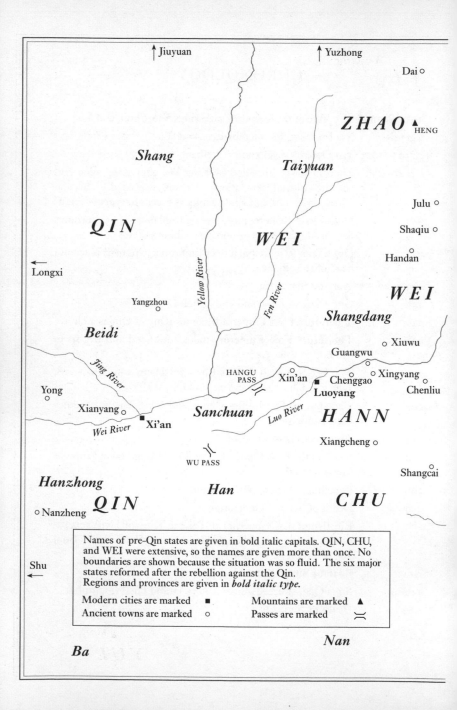

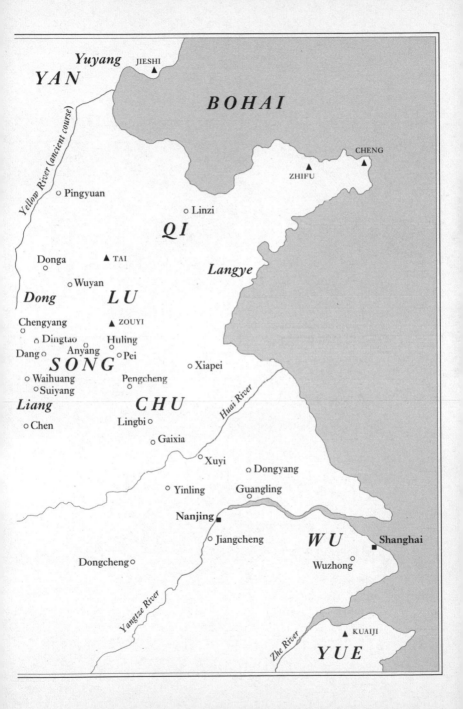

THE FIRST EMPEROR

1

THE BIRTH OF THE FIRST EMPEROR

I start these translations with a rendering of the biography of the famous merchant Lü Buwei (chapter 85 of the Historical Records), which provides the source for believing that he was the father of the First Emperor of Qin. The story begins in the fortieth year of the reign of King Zhaoxiang, which was 267 BC.

LÜ BUWEI was an important merchant from Yangdi. As he travelled about, he bought cheap and sold dear, and his household amassed a fortune worth thousands of *jin.**

In the fortieth year of King Zhaoxiang of Qin the Crown Prince died. In his forty-second year his next son, Lord Anguo, was made crown prince. Lord Anguo had more than twenty sons. He had a concubine whom he especially loved so that he immediately made her his chief consort, and she was entitled the Lady Huayang. But she was childless. One of Lord Anguo's sons was called Zichu, and his mother, the concubine Xia, was not loved. Zichu became a hostage-son* of Qin in Zhao. Qin frequently attacked Zhao, so Zhao did not treat Zichu with very much ceremony.

As a grandson of the ruler of Qin and the son of a concubine sent as hostage to another state, Zichu was not liberally supplied with carriages and other resources, but dwelt in harsh conditions and could not get what he wanted. Lü Buwei was in Handan* on business, and when he met him he felt pity for him. 'This rare commodity should be invested in,' he said. Accordingly he went to see Zichu. 'I can make your establishment grand,' he said. Zichu laughed. 'You should make your own establishment grand, and then afterwards make mine grand!' he exclaimed. 'You are not getting the point,' said Lü Buwei. 'To become grand my establishment depends on yours.'

Zichu at heart understood what he meant, so he led him off to sit with him and talk frankly. 'The King of Qin has grown old,' said Lü Buwei, 'and Lord Anguo has managed to become crown prince.

I hear that Lord Anguo is especially fond of the Lady Huayang, but she is childless. But the only one who can establish a successor is the Lady Huayang. Now you, sir, have more than twenty brothers and, what is more, you occupy only a middling position among them, so that you are not highly favoured, and for a long time you have been held hostage in another state. When the Great King passes away and Lord Anguo is set up as king, you have no prospect of being able to contend for the position of crown prince with the elder sons and all those sons who are in his presence morning and evening.'

'Yes,' said Zichu, 'but what am I to do about it?' 'You, sir, are poor and a stranger here,' said Lü Buwei, 'and it is not the case that you possess the means to offer gifts to relatives or secure pledges of support from visitors. Although I am poor, I beg to journey west for you with 1,000 *jin* and, through serving Lord Anguo and Lady Huayang, establish you as their heir.' So Zichu bowed. 'It will surely turn out as you plan,' he said, 'and I beg to be able to divide up the state of Qin and share it with you.'

Lü Buwei then gave Zichu 500 *jin* for his expenses and to secure pledges of support,* and spent a further 500 *jin* on curiosities and trinkets. At his own expense he journeyed westward to Qin and sought an interview with the elder sister of the Lady Huayang, so that she might present all such objects to the Lady Huayang. He took advantage of the opportunity to speak of Zichu's talent and wisdom and mentioned how he had secured pledges of support in the various states. As he travelled the world, he was always saying: 'I think of the Lady as Heaven. Day and night I weep as I think of the Crown Prince and the Lady.'

The Lady was highly delighted, so Buwei got her elder sister to tell her: 'I have heard that, in the case of one who serves a man through beauty, when the beauty fades the love will decline. Now you serve the Crown Prince, and although you are much loved, you are childless; so, if you do not lose this opportunity to reach an early agreement with one of the princes who is talented and filial, and immediately establish him as heir and make him your son, while your husband is alive you will be deeply honoured and, after his sad loss, when the one whom you have made son becomes king, you will definitely not lose your power, and this is what is meant by "profit for ten thousand generations deriving from a single word". If you do not plant roots while there are abundant flowers,* then as soon as your beauty fades and love has declined, even if you wanted to utter a single word, could this still be achieved? Now Zichu is a man of quality, but he realizes that he is a middle son and cannot become the heir because of his inferior rank, and his mother, too, is not favoured, so he has attached himself to Your Ladyship, and if you really take this opportunity to pick him out and make him heir, then Your Ladyship will receive favour from Qin until the end of your life.'

The Lady Huayang thought this was true and, seizing an opportunity when the Crown Prince was taking his ease, she calmly told him that Zichu, who had been taken as a hostage by Zhao, was extremely talented, and was praised by all who travelled about. Then she wept because of this. 'I have been lucky to have been able to occupy a position in your harem,' she said, 'but unlucky to have no son. I would like to get Zichu immediately established as your successor, so that I may entrust my life to him.' Lord Anguo agreed to this, and so he gave the Lady an engraved jade tally* to guarantee that he would be appointed as successor. Lord Anguo and the Lady accordingly sent generous presents to Zichu and requested that Lü Buwei would tutor him. Because of this, Zichu's reputation thrived increasingly in the feudal states.

Lü Buwei had taken to live with him the most attractive among all the courtesans of Handan, who was also good at dancing. He became aware that she was pregnant. When Zichu was drinking with Buwei he saw her and took a fancy to her, and so he got up to propose a toast and asked for her. Lü Buwei was angry but, recalling that he had already ruined his estate for Zichu's sake, and intended to fish for something marvellous as a result of this, he accordingly made a present of his concubine, and she concealed her pregnancy. When her time at long last came,* she gave birth to a son, Zheng. Zichu then made the concubine his wife.

In the fiftieth year of King Zhaoxiang of Qin, Wang Yi was dispatched to lay siege to Handan; and, when the pressure was intensified, Zhao wanted to kill Zichu. Having discussed the matter with Lü Buwei, Zichu obtained his release by distributing 600 catties of gold to the officers who were guarding him. He disappeared, and made his way to the Qin army and so in this way he was able to get back home. Zhao intended to kill Zichu's wife and child but, as she was the daughter of a powerful family in Zhao, she was able to go into hiding, and for this reason both mother and son were in the end able to survive. In the fifty-sixth year of his reign King Zhaoxiang of Qin passed away, and the Crown Prince, Lord Anguo, was set up as king, and the Lady Huayang became queen and Zichu became crown prince. Zhao also arranged for Zichu's wife and son, Zheng, to be sent home to Qin.

One year after he was set on the throne the King of Qin passed away. His posthumous name* was King Xiaowen. Crown Prince Zichu was set on the throne in his place, and he was to become King Zhuangxiang. The one whom King Zhuangxiang had treated as mother became Queen Dowager Huayang and his real mother, Lady Xia, was honoured with the title of Queen Dowager Xia. In the first year of King Zhuangxiang, Lü Buwei was appointed chief minister and enfeoffed as Marquis of Wenxin, to enjoy the revenues from 100,000 households in Henan and Luoyang.

Three years after he ascended the throne King Zhuangxiang passed away and Crown Prince Zheng was set up as king. He honoured Lü Buwei by making him chief minister, and entitled him 'uncle'.* Since the King of Qin was young, the Queen Dowager from time to time had illicit relations in secret with Lü Buwei. And Buwei had a myriad household servants.

At this time there flourished Lord Xinling* in Wei, Lord Chunshen in Chu, Lord Pingyuan in Zhao, and Lord Mengchang in Qi, all of whom had men of action under them and took delight in entertaining visitors so as to subvert each other. On account of the strength of Qin, Lü Buwei was ashamed at not being equal to them, and so he also welcomed men of action and treated them generously. Thus he attracted dependants to the number of 3,000 men. At this time in the various states there were many disputants, for example people like Xun Qing,* and the books they wrote spread throughout the world. So Lü Buwei made each of his dependants write down what he had learnt, and their combined observations were made into eight surveys, six discussions, and twelve records, more than 200,000 words in all. He thought that this gave a complete account of everything in Heaven and Earth and of matters both ancient and modern, and it was called the *Springs and Autumns of Lü.** It was displayed at the gateway of Xianyang market, and 1,000 *jin* were hung above it. Itinerant scholars and dependants of the rulers of the various states were invited, and anyone of them who could add or subtract a single word was to be given 1,000 *jin*.

The First Emperor* was growing up, but the Queen Dowager's immoral behaviour did not cease. Lü Buwei was afraid that disaster would befall himself if they were discovered, so he secretly sought out Lao Ai, a man with a large penis, and made him a retainer. Sometimes, to the strains of licentious music, he made Lao Ai walk along with a wheel of *tong*-wood attached to his penis, and he ensured that the Queen Dowager heard about it so that she might be tempted. And when she heard, she did indeed want to get hold of him in private. Lü Buwei accordingly presented Lao Ai, but fraudulently got someone to report him for a crime that merited castration. Buwei then told the Queen Dowager on the quiet: 'If it were possible to perform a bogus castration, then he could be handed over to serve in the palace.'

The Queen Dowager accordingly paid generous bribes on the quiet to the officer in charge of castration and, when Lao Ai had been falsely condemned, his beard and eyebrows were plucked out so that he could play the part of an eunuch, and consequently he was able to serve the Queen Dowager. The Queen Dowager secretly had intercourse with him and became extremely fond of him. Becoming pregnant, the Queen Dowager feared that other people would become aware of it, so she pretended that an oracle had said that she ought to withdraw for a time, so she left the palace to reside at Yong. Lao Ai was in constant attendance and she was extremely generous in her rewards, and matters were all decided by Lao Ai, who had several thousand household servants, and more than 1,000 of the various aliens who sought official positions became retainers of Lao Ai.

In the seventh year* of the First Emperor, King Zhuangxiang's mother, the Queen Dowager Xia, passed away. The consort of King Xiaowen, known as Queen Dowager Huayang, was buried in the same grave as King Xiaowen at Shouling. Since Queen Dowager Xia's son King Zhuangxiang was buried at Zhiyang, consequently

Queen Dowager Xia* had made arrangements for herself to be buried separately east of Du, saying: 'On the east I shall gaze towards my son, and on the west I shall gaze towards my husband. In 100 years' time there ought to be a city of 10,000 households at my side.'

In the ninth year of the First Emperor there was a report that Lao Ai was really not an eunuch and that he regularly indulged in secret improprieties with the Queen Dowager, who had given birth to two children, both of whom had been concealed. He had plotted with the Queen Dowager, saying: 'Once the King passes away, we will make our son succeed.' At that the King of Qin handed him over to the law officers for trial and, when all the facts had been obtained, Chief Minister Lü Buwei was implicated in the affair. In the ninth month Lao Ai was wiped out with all his kinsmen, and the two children born of the Queen Dowager were put to death, and then the Queen Dowager was removed to Yong. All Lao Ai's retainers lost their property and were deported to Shu.* The King had intended to condemn Lü Buwei to death, but because of the greatness of the services that he had performed for his predecessor, together with the fact that the visitors and disputants who spoke up on his behalf as they travelled about were numerous, the King could not bear to bring the law on him.

In the tenth month of the tenth year of the King of Qin, Lü Buwei was dismissed from being chief minister. When Mao Jiao, a man of Qi, advised accordingly, the King of Qin welcomed the Queen Dowager back from Yong and restored her to Xianyang and sent Lü Buwei, as Marquis of Wenxin, off to his fief in Henan.

After just over a year visitors and emissaries from the various states were always in sight of each other on the road as they took invitations to the Marquis of Wenxin. The King of Qin was afraid that they were making a revolt, so he bestowed a letter on the Marquis of Wenxin saying: 'What have you achieved for Qin that Qin should have enfeoffed you in Henan to enjoy the revenue from 100,000 households? What intimacy have you shown towards Qin that you should be entitled "uncle"? You are to remove yourself together with your family and followers and go and live in Shu!' Lü Buwei reckoned that he was gradually being put under pressure and was afraid that he would be sentenced to death, so he drank poison and died. Once Lü Buwei and Lao Ai, with whom the King of Qin had grown increasingly angry, were both dead, he recalled all Lao Ai's retainers who had been deported to Shu.

In the nineteenth year of the First Emperor, the Queen Dowager passed away. She was given the posthumous title of Empress Dowager, and she was buried in the same grave as King Zhuangxiang at Zhiyang.

The Grand Historiographer* says: 'Buwei and Lao Ai were honoured, and the former was enfeoffed as Marquis of Wenxin. When somebody reported Lao Ai, Ai heard about it. But when the King of Qin interrogated those close to him, the truth was not yet revealed. But when the Supreme One* went to Yong to perform the sacrifice at the bounds, Lao Ai was afraid that disaster would arise, and so he plotted together with his clique to pretend that he had the Queen Dowager's authority and to send troops to bring about an uprising at Qinian palace. But officers were sent to attack Ai, who was defeated and fled. He was pursued and beheaded at Haozhi, and subsequently his clan was wiped out. And it was in consequence of this that Lü Buwei was driven out. What Master Kong meant by "the man of reputation"* surely refers to Master Lü?'

2

AN ASSASSINATION ATTEMPT

In 227 BC, not long before the Qin unification of China, a famous assassination attempt on the ruler of Qin and later First Emperor of China was made by Jing Ke, whose story is recorded in chapter 86 of the Historical Records, *which is a collective biography of assassins. It reads as follows:*

JING KE was a man of Wey.* His forebears were in fact people from Qi, but they had migrated to Wey, and the Wey people called him 'the noble Qing'. But he went to Yan and the Yan people called him 'the noble Jing'.

The noble Jing was fond of reading and swordsmanship, and he spoke about his skills to Lord Yuan of Wey, but Lord Yuan did not employ him. After this, when Qin attacked Wei and established the Dong Province, Lord Yuan's relatives were removed to Yewang.

Jing Ke once visited Yuci on his travels, and he discussed swordsmanship with Ge Nie, but Ge Nie grew angry and glared at him. When Jing Ke left, someone suggested calling him back. 'When I was discussing swordsmanship with him just now,' said Ge Nie, 'something disagreeable happened, so I glared at him; if he is endeavouring to go on his journey, it is right that he should leave, and I shall not presume to detain him.' A messenger was sent to the traveller's host, but Jing Ke had already harnessed his horse to his carriage and left Yuci. When the messenger returned and made his report, Ge Nie said: 'To be sure, he has gone, for just now I put him right with a glare.'

When Jing Ke was in Handan on his travels, Lu Goujian was playing *bo** with him. They fell out and Lu Goujian grew angry and shouted at him. Jing Ke made off in silence, and after that they did not meet again.

When Jing Ke reached Yan, he became fond of a dog-butcher from Yan and also Gao Jianli who was a skilled lute-player. Jing Ke was addicted to wine, and every day he had a drink in the market-place at the Yan capital with the dog-butcher and Gao Jianli. After they got drunk, Gao Jianli played the lute and Jing Ke sang in harmony with him in the market-place; and as they had taken their pleasures together, so when they finished they wept together as if there were nobody else about. Although Jing Ke frequented the company of winebibbers, nevertheless he was a man who was serious-minded and fond of reading; and in all the states to which he travelled, he and all the men of quality, enterprise, and seniority in those places became involved with each other. And when he went to Yan, a public servant living in retirement called Master Tian Guang also treated him well because he appreciated that he was not an ordinary person.

After a while it so happened that Crown Prince Dan of Yan, who had been held hostage in Qin, escaped and returned to Yan. Crown Prince Dan of Yan had once in the past been held hostage by Zhao and, as King Zheng of Qin was born in Zhao,* he had got on well with Dan when they were young. But when Zheng was set up as King of Qin, Dan was made hostage by Qin. And when the King of Qin's treatment of Crown Prince Dan of Yan deteriorated, Dan, becoming resentful in consequence, fled back home. After his return he sought someone who would take vengeance on the King of Qin for him, for the state was small and did not have the strength to be able to do so. Later on Qin daily sent out soldiers east of the mountains to attack Qi, Chu, and the three successor states of Jin,* and gradually nibbled away at the feudal states. When they were just about to reach Yan, both the ruler of Yan and his ministers were afraid that disaster would befall. Crown Prince Dan was worried about this and consulted his tutor, Ju Wu. 'The territory of Qin spreads throughout all under Heaven,'* Wu replied, 'and it is menacing Hann, Wei, and Zhao. In the north it has gained possession of the strongholds of Ganquan and Gukou, and in the south it has gained possession of the fertile lands beside the Jing and the Wei. It exploits the abundance of Ba and Han. To the west it has the mountains of Long and Shu, and to the east it has the difficult terrain of the pass and of Xiao. Its people are multitudinous, its officers well disciplined, and it has a superabundance of weapons and armour. As far as he has revealed his intentions, there is nothing yet settled about the area south of the Great Wall and north of the River Yi.* Why do you want to raise her hackles because of resentment at having been insulted?' 'In that case, what course shall I follow?' said Dan. 'I beg to go inside and ponder this,' he replied.

After a while the Qin general Fan Yuqi gave offence to the King of Qin, so he fled and went to Yan, where the Crown Prince received him and provided him with somewhere to stay. 'It should not be done,' remonstrated Ju Wu. 'If anger is concentrated on Yan because of the bad temper of the King of Qin, that is enough to turn one's heart cold, so how much the more will this be so if he hears where General Fan is? This is what is meant by "casting meat in the path of a hungry tiger", for disaster will certainly become inescapable. Even if Guan and Yan* were alive, they could not make plans to deal with this. I wish that Your Highness would quickly dispatch General Fan to the Xiongnu* in order that he may be silenced. I respectfully suggest that in the west you reach an agreement with the three successor states of Jin, and in the south you link up with Qi and Chu, and in the north you get on terms with the Khan, and after this plans can indeed be made.'

'Your scheme, Grand Tutor, is time-consuming,' said the Crown Prince. 'It will take ages. But I am rather stupid, and I am afraid I cannot wait a moment. Moreover it is not only to do with this. That General Fan, at large in the world in a desperate situation, put himself into my care, and I certainly will not, just because I am persecuted by a powerful Qin, abandon a relationship with someone I have taken pity on and hand him over to the Xiongnu. This is an absolutely crucial time for me. I would like you, Grand Tutor, to think about it again.'

Ju Wu said: 'Intending to seek peace while one does dangerous things, seeking good fortune while one is constructing disaster, feeling deep resentment while one is making shallow plans, binding oneself to future association with a single person and not concerning oneself with the great harm which will befall the state, this is what is meant by "assisting disaster by building up a stock of resentment". If wild swan's feathers are burnt on the charcoal in a stove, there is certainly nothing to be done about it. Similarly if cruel anger is brought into action by a hawk-like Qin, the consequences are surely not worth talking about. In Yan there is Mr Tian Guang, who is a man of profound wisdom and steeped in courage. You should make plans with him.' 'I should like to avail myself of your assistance, Grand Tutor, to make the acquaintance of Mr Tian,' said the Crown Prince. 'Would that be possible?' 'With respect, I promise to arrange this,' said Ju Wu. He left and went to see Mr Tian, and said: 'The Crown Prince wishes advice on affairs of state to be given by you, sir.' 'I respectfully accept these instructions,' said Tian Guang. Accordingly he went to see him.

When receiving him the Crown Prince stood to one side to conduct him in, knelt down, and dusted the mat.* When Tian Guang was settled in his place and there was nobody else present, the Crown Prince left his mat and requested: 'Yan and Qin will not stand as two, and I would like you, sir, to let your thoughts dwell on this.' 'Your servant has heard', said Tian Guang, 'that when a fine horse is in its prime, it gallops 1,000 *li* in one day; but when it grows old and feeble, a wornout nag gets ahead of it. Now Your Highness has heard about me as I was when I was in my prime, and he is not aware that my skill has already melted away. Nevertheless, although I do not venture to use it to give advice on affairs of state, Jing Ke, of whom I think highly, should be used for this mission.' 'I should like to avail myself of your assistance, sir, to get acquainted with Jing Ke,' said the Crown Prince. 'Is that possible?' 'With respect, I promise to arrange this,' said Tian Guang.

Straightway he rose and hurried out. The Crown Prince saw him off and, when they reached the gate, he warned: 'What I have reported and what you have said are important matters of state, so I would like you, sir, not to let them leak out.' 'I promise,' said Tian Guang, bowing and smiling. Walking quickly, he went to see Jing Ke. 'You and I think well of each other,' he said, 'as everyone in Yan knows. Now the Crown Prince has heard of me as I was in my prime and is not aware that physically I am no longer up to it, so he has done me the honour of instructing me: "Yan and Qin will not stand as two, and I would like you, sir, to let your thoughts dwell on this." Despite my humility I did not rule myself out completely, but mentioned you, sir, to the Crown Prince. I would like you, sir, to call on the Crown Prince at the palace.' 'I shall respectfully accept your instructions,' said Jing Ke. 'I have heard', said Tian Guang, 'that when a venerable person undertakes some action, he does not cause others to be suspicious of him. Now when the Crown Prince told me, "What we talked about were important matters of state, and I would like you, sir, not to let them leak out," this was due to the fact that the Crown Prince was suspicious of me. Now if one undertakes some action but causes other people to be suspicious of one, this is neither moral nor brave.' Intending to kill himself so as to inspire Jing Ke, he said: 'I would like you, sir, to go urgently and call on the Crown Prince, and mention that Guang is already dead, to make it clear that he will not talk.' Accordingly he cut his throat and died.*

Jing Ke then went to see the Crown Prince, mentioned that Tian Guang had died, and passed on what he had said. The Crown Prince bowed twice and knelt down, and wept as he crawled along. After a moment he said: 'The reason why I warned Master Tian not to say anything was because I wished by doing so to bring to completion the planning of a great enterprise. That Master Tian should now make it clear that he would not talk by dying, was surely not my intention!'

When Jing Ke's place had been arranged, the Crown Prince left his mat and bowed. 'Mr Tian was not aware that I am unworthy,' he said, 'so he made it possible for you to come into my presence so that I could venture to have something to say. This is how Heaven shows pity for Yan and will not discard me when I succeed to the throne. Now Qin has a heart which is greedy for profit, and its desires are insatiable. If it does not absorb all the land under Heaven, and make all the kings within the seas its subjects, its ambitions will not be satisfied. At the present time Qin has already taken captive the King of Hann, and has annexed all his territories. It has also raised troops to attack Chu in the south and threatens Zhao in the north. Wang Jian is leading a host of several hundred thousand to confront Zhang and Ye, and Li Xin has sallied forth towards Taiyuan and Yunzhong. Zhao cannot withstand Qin, and is bound to submit and become its vassal, and if it does so then calamity will befall Yan. Yan is small and weak and has frequently been harassed by soldiers, so now I reckon that the whole state would be an inadequate match for Qin. If the feudal states are submitting to Qin, nobody will dare to form a north–south alliance.* As for my own secret plan, I foolishly consider that, if we can really get hold of the bravest man of action* under Heaven and send him on a mission to Qin to provide a glimpse of substantial profit, the King of Qin will be greedy for it, and with his power he makes a point of getting whatever he wants. If we really succeed in putting pressure on the King of Qin to make him restore all the territory of the feudal states he has usurped, as in the case of Cao Mo* and Duke Huan of Qi, then it will be splendid. But if this is impossible, he shall consequently be stabbed to death. Those important generals of Qin have full responsibility for troops deployed in the field, so when there is chaos in the capital there will be mutual suspicion between ruler and ruled; and through the opportunity provided by this the feudal states will be able to form north–south alliances, and it will become inevitable that they defeat Qin. This is my supreme desire, but I do not know to whom to entrust our fate. It is up to you, Jing Ke, to let your thoughts dwell on this.'

'This is an important affair of state,' said Jing Ke after a long time, 'and I am a jaded creature. I am afraid I am not fit to be entrusted with the mission.' Only after the Crown Prince had bowed before him and earnestly begged him not to hold back did he agree. Then Jing Ke was honoured as a senior minister and lodged in superior accommodation. The Crown Prince went daily to his gate and provided him with the paraphernalia of the grand sacrifice, and unusual objects were handed in at intervals, and carriages, horsemen, and beautiful women were provided to satisfy Jing Ke's desires, so as to smooth the path of his intentions.

For a long time Jing Ke never had the intention of making the journey. The Qin general Wang Jian defeated Zhao and captured the King of Zhao, and annexed the whole of its territory. He advanced his troops to capture territory to the north and arrived at the southern borders of Yan. Crown Prince Dan was terrified and so he implored Jing Ke. 'Since any moment now the Qin troops will cross the River Yi,' he said, 'even if I wished to go on supporting you, sir, surely that could not be done!' 'Even if Your Highness had not spoken,' said Jing Ke, 'your servant wanted to pay you a visit. If I make the journey now but do not have evidence of good faith, the King of Qin will be quite unapproachable. But as for General Fan, the King of Qin has offered 1,000 catties of gold and a city of 10,000 households for him. If I were actually to get hold of General Fan's head together with a map of Dukang* in Yan, and took them and presented them to the King of Qin, the King of Qin would certainly be pleased to grant me audience, and I would indeed be able to have something to report.' 'General Fan came and took refuge with me when he was in dire distress,' said the Crown Prince, 'and although I cannot bear to harm the purposes of a venerable person such as yourself because of a private matter of my own, I would like you, sir, to reflect on this again!'

Knowing that the Crown Prince could not bear to go along with this, he then went and saw Fan Yuqi in private. 'The way Qin has treated you, general, may be described as atrocious,' he said. 'Your father and mother and your kinsmen were all put to death because of you. Now I hear that a price of 1,000 catties of gold and a city of 10,000 households has been put on your head. What will you do about it?' Yuqi gazed up to Heaven, sighed heavily, and wept. 'Every time I remember this,' he said, 'I always suffer pain to the very marrow of my bones; but when I make plans, I do not know what to come up with, and that is all there is to it.' 'If I have a single utterance which may relieve the state of Yan from distress and take vengeance on your enemies, general, what about it?' said Jing Ke. 'What is to be done about it then?' said Yuqi coming forward. 'I would like to get hold of your head, general, so as to present it to the King of Qin,' said Jing Ke. The King of Qin is bound to be pleased and grant me an audience, and I will grab his sleeve with my left hand and stab him in the chest with my right hand. In that case vengeance will be wreaked on your enemy, and Yan's shame at having been insulted will be removed. But you would surely not be willing?'

Fan Yuqi strode forward, baring one shoulder and clasping his wrist.* 'This is what I have been grinding my teeth and wearying my heart over with rage day and night,' he said. 'And now I have actually been able to hear some advice!' Then he slit his throat. When the Crown Prince heard about it, he went over quickly, prostrated himself in front of the corpse and wept, and felt extremely remorseful. But since in the event there was nothing else that could be done, he then put Fan Yuqi's head in a casket and sealed it.

Thereupon the Crown Prince, in preparation for the mission, sought the sharpest dagger in the world and obtained one from Xu Furen, a man of Zhao, who took 100 *jin* for it. He made a craftsman coat it with poison so as to try it out on other people, and although the blood drawn only caused a slight stain, all the people died instantaneously. Accordingly it was packed in the luggage being got ready for Jing Ke's journey. In the state of Yan there was a bold fellow named Qin Wuyang, who had committed murder although he was only 13 years old, and people did not dare look him in the eye. So Qin Wuyang was ordered to become his assistant.

But there was someone else Jing Ke was waiting for, since he intended to take him along with him. The person in question lived at a distance and had not yet come, so he made preparations for the journey on his behalf. After a while, since he had not yet set out, the Crown Prince thought that he was procrastinating and suspected that he had changed his mind and was feeling regretful, so he put a further request: 'The days are already getting used up,' he said, 'and surely you have no intention of going. I beg to be able to send Qin Wuyang ahead.' Jing Ke was furious. 'Why should you send him?' he shouted at the Crown Prince. 'That silly fellow would be the one who would set out and not return. What is more, I shall be entering Qin, which is immeasurably powerful, having picked up a single dagger, and the reason for my delay is that I am waiting for my friend to come with me. If Your Highness thinks I am procrastinating, I beg to take my leave this instant.' And so he set out.

The Crown Prince and those of his visitors who were aware of what was going on all put on white mourning clothes* and cap to see him off. When he reached the banks of the River Yi, he set out on his way after they had sacrificed to the Spirit of the Road. Gao Jianli played the lute, and Jing Ke sang in harmony. They made a mournful sound and the gentlemen present all shed tears. Then he stepped forward and performed a song which went

> The wind sighs and the River Yi is cold.
> Once the brave fellow leaves,
> He will not return again.

Afterwards they performed a stirring tune,* and the gentlemen present all wore looks of anger, and their hair all bristled up, pushing at their caps. Then Jing Ke went over to the carriage and set off, and he did not look back at all.

Next they reached Qin and, taking gifts worth 1,000 *jin*, made a generous present to Meng Jia, a palace cadet who was a favourite official of the King of Qin. Jia first spoke to the King of Qin on his behalf. 'The King of Yan is truly alarmed at the Great King's awesomeness,' he said, 'and does not dare to raise troops in order to resist the officers of your army. He wishes the whole state to become a vassal and join the ranks of the other states in presenting tribute and acting like provinces and districts, so as to be able to have the honour to protect the ancestral temples of the previous kings. In his terror he does not dare to present himself, but he has respectfully cut off Fan Yuqi's head and with it presents a map of Dukang in Yan, put in a casket and sealed up. With his salutations, the King of Yan dispatched these things from the audience chamber and has sent an emissary to report to the Great King. It is for the Great King to give him instructions about this.'

When the King of Qin heard this, he was highly delighted and, putting on court dress, arranged a grand levee, and gave audience to the Yan emissary in the palace at Xianyang. Jing Ke offered the casket containing Fan Yuqi's head and Qin Wuyang offered the map-case, going forward one after the other. When they reached the steps, Qin Wuyang changed colour and trembled with fear, and all the officials were surprised at him. Jing Ke turned and laughed at Wuyang. He went forward and apologized. 'He is a rustic fellow from the barbarians of the northern frontier,' he said, 'and he has never once set eyes on the Son of Heaven,* so he is trembling with fear. I would like the Great King to be a little lenient with him, to enable us to complete our mission in his presence.'

'Get hold of the map which Wuyang is carrying,' said the King of Qin. When Jing Ke had got hold of the map and offered it to him, the King of Qin unrolled the map. And when the map was completely unrolled, the dagger was revealed. Using his left hand, he grabbed the King of Qin's sleeve, and with his right hand he held the dagger to stab him. But before it reached his body the King of Qin drew back in alarm and rose to his feet, and the sleeve tore off. He tried to draw his sword, but his sword was long and got stuck in the scabbard.

At the time he was agitated and so, as the sword was rigid, it could not be drawn immediately.

Jing Ke pursued the King of Qin, but the King of Qin fled round a pillar. The officials were all startled and suddenly rose to their feet in the face of the unexpected, and became completely disorganized. Moreover, according to Qin law, all the officials who served at the top of the hall could not carry even the tiniest weapon, and all the palace gentlemen bearing weapons were paraded at the foot of the hall, and except when there was a summons by imperial edict, they could not come up to the top of the hall. So just at the moment of emergency, he did not get around to summoning the soldiers down below, and that was why Jing Ke actually pursued the King of Qin. And he in his sudden agitation, having nothing else with which to strike Ke, thrust at him with hands joined together.

At this time the attendant physician, Xia Wuju, warded off Jing Ke with the bag in which he carried drugs. The King of Qin had just fled round the pillar and in his sudden agitation he did not know what he was doing, so his courtiers said: 'Put the sword behind you, Your Majesty.' When the sword had been put behind him, he then drew it and struck Jing Ke with it, and he cut his left thigh. Jing Ke was finished, but he drew back his dagger to hurl it at the King of Qin. However, he missed and hit the bronze pillar. The King of Qin again struck at Jing Ke and Ke suffered eight wounds. Ke himself realized that the enterprise had failed, so he leant on the pillar and laughed. He cursed as he sprawled with his legs spread out. 'The reason why the job is unfinished', he said, 'is because I intended to take him by force while he was still alive, and insist on getting the compact in order to repay the Crown Prince.' Thereupon, when the courtiers had come forward to kill Ke, the King of Qin remained embarrassed for a good long while. Eventually, when he discussed achievements there were discrepancies in both the rewarding of the various officials and in the question of those who ought to be tried, but he bestowed 200 *yi** of gold on Xia Wuju. 'Wuju loves me,' he said, 'so he warded Jing Ke off with his bag of drugs.'

Thereupon the King of Qin in his great rage sent forth more and more soldiers to go to Zhao and decreed that Wang Jian's army should attack Yan. In ten months they took the city of Ji.*

Xi King of Yan, Crown Prince Dan, and the rest, at the head of all their élite troops, went eastwards to find security in Liaodong.* General Li Xin of Qin pursued and smote them and the King of Yan was hard-pressed, and Jia King of Dai then sent Xi King of Yan a letter. 'The reason why Qin is pursuing Yan all the more relentlessly is because of Crown Prince Dan,' it said. 'Now if the King were really to kill Dan and present him to the King of Qin, the King of Qin would be bound to break off, and your altars of land and grain would fortunately be able to receive their sacrifices.' After this Li Xin pursued Dan and Dan went into hiding in the area of the River Yan.* The King of Yan accordingly sent messengers to cut off Crown Prince Dan's head, intending to present it to Qin. But Qin again made soldiers advance and attack them. Five years later Qin troops wiped out Yan and took Xi King of Yan prisoner.

The following year Qin unified all under Heaven and the title of August Emperor* was immediately adopted. Then Qin pursued the friends of Crown Prince Dan and Jing Ke and they all vanished. Gao Jianli changed his name and became a hired servant, and hid himself away in Songzi. After a long time, having lived a hard life, he heard a guest playing the lute in the hall of the house where he was a servant, so he hung about and could not go away. Every time he blurted out the remark that 'There is good and bad in that,' the attendants reported this to their master. 'That hireling really does understand music,' they said. 'On the quiet he is saying what is right and wrong.' The head of the household summoned him into his presence to play the lute, and the whole assembled company praised his skill and bestowed wine upon him. But Gao Jianli, reflecting on the fact that he had long been in hiding and had spent an endless period of fear and hardship, accordingly withdrew and got out his lute and his best clothes from his luggage, and came into their presence again with his appearance transformed. The assembled guests were all astonished and, ignoring the requirements of ceremony, they subordinated themselves to him and treated him as the guest of honour. They got him to play the lute and sing, and all the guests were in tears when they left. The story of his being treated as a guest was passed on in Songzi, and was heard by the First Emperor of Qin. When the First Emperor summoned him to audience, someone recognized him, and so he said: 'It is Gao Jianli.' The August Emperor of Qin was so moved by his excellent lute-playing that he gave him a special pardon and merely put out his eyes. When he got him to play the lute he always praised his skill. Gradually he let him come closer, so Gao Jianli weighted the lute with lead, and when he next came in and got close, he raised the lute to strike the August Emperor of Qin, but missed. Thereupon he had Gao Jianli put to death, and for the rest of his life he did not again allow anyone from the feudal states to come close to him.

When Lu Goujian heard that Jing Ke had tried to stab the King of Qin, he said in private: 'Alas, what a pity he did not make a proper study of the art of swordsmanship! How thoroughly I misunderstand people! Once upon a time I shouted at him, but he has indeed made me into a nonentity.'

The Grand Historiographer said: 'Contemporary accounts of the Jing Ke story, which refer to Crown Prince Dan's command that "Heaven should rain grain and horses should grow horns",* are grossly misleading. To say that Jing Ke wounded the King of Qin is also quite wrong. Right at the start Gongsun Jigong and Master Dong used to enjoy spending their spare time with Xia Wuju, and they became aware of everything that happened, and they told it to me* just like this.

'From Cao Mo to Jing Ke* some of these five men fulfilled their duty and some did not, but it is quite clear that they had made up their minds. They did not betray their purposes, so surely it is not absurd that their names should be handed down to posterity.'

3

THE BIOGRAPHY OF
THE CHIEF MINISTER OF QIN

We now move on to the biography of Li Si (chapter 87), a very important politician during the Qin Dynasty. The chapter starts with an account of his early days, and covers some of the events leading up to the establishment of the Qin Dynasty.

Li Si was a man of Shangcai in Chu. In his youth, when he was a minor clerk in the province, he noticed rats eating filth in the latrines of the clerks' hostel; and if they approached a man or a dog, they were generally scared of them. But when Si entered a granary, he observed that the rats in the granary were eating the stored-up grain, living underneath the main chamber of the granary, and not being worried by either man or dog. At this Li Si sighed and said: 'A man's status is just the same as with rats. It simply depends on where one locates oneself!'

He thereupon became a follower of Xun Qing and studied the techniques of emperorhood and kingship. When his studies had been completed, reckoning that the King of Chu was not worth serving and that the Six States* were all weak and that none of them was fit to have meritorious deeds done for it, he intended to travel westwards and enter Qin. Taking leave of Xun Qing, he said: 'I have heard that if one gets an opportunity one should not be slow to seize it. At the present time, when the 10,000 chariots* are on the verge of combat, itinerant advisers are in control of affairs. The King of Qin now intends to swallow up all under Heaven and govern with the title of emperor.* This is the moment for a commoner to bestir himself and indeed a ripe opportunity for an itinerant adviser. If one stays in a humble position and decides not to take action, this is to behave like an animal, whose only concern is food. Only if one has a human countenance is one capable of taking vigorous action. Hence there is no greater disgrace than lowliness and no deeper sorrow than poverty. To stay in a humble position for a long time or live in an area which suffers distress, to reject the age and show a hatred of profit, and to commit oneself to a lack of purposive activity*—this is not the nature of a man of action. Therefore I intend to travel westwards and act as adviser to the King of Qin.'

Having reached Qin just when King Zhuangxiang had died, Li Si sought to become a member of the household of Lü Buwei, Marquis of Wenxin, the Chief Minister of Qin. Buwei regarded him as a man of quality and appointed him a palace gentleman.* Accordingly Li Si was able to offer advice, so he told the King of Qin: 'The ordinary person misses his chances. The completion of great enterprises consists of taking advantage of weaknesses and ruthlessly exploiting them. Why is it that in former times when Duke Mu of Qin was paramount prince he absolutely failed to move east and annex the area of the Six States?* The feudal lords were still numerous and the virtue* of Zhou had not yet gone into a decline, so the five hegemons* rose up one after the other and still honoured the house of Zhou. But from the time of Duke Xiao of Qin onwards the house of Zhou went into a decline and the feudal states annexed each other, so that the area east of the passes became the Six States, and it has taken just six reigns* for Qin, as a result of its victories, to make the feudal states subservient. Now the feudal states are submissive towards Qin and are just like provinces and districts.

'Now if one takes into account the strength of Qin and the Great King's own fine qualities, it will be capable not only of wiping out the feudal states just as easily as sweeping the top of a stove, but also of completing the imperial heritage and making all under Heaven into a unity. This is the one opportunity in 10,000 generations. If you are idle and do not press ahead, the feudal states will regain their strength and will combine with each other to form north–south alliances, and even if you had the fine qualities of the Yellow Emperor you would not be able to unify them.'

The King of Qin thereupon appointed Si a senior scribe and, heeding his advice, secretly dispatched conspirators bearing gold and jade to act as itinerant advisers to the feudal lords. And any of the famous public servants in the feudal states who could be subverted with bribes were brought into collusion with generous gifts; and those who refused were stabbed with sharp swords. They created rifts in policy between rulers and their ministers, and the King of Qin then sent his finest generals to follow in their rear. The King of Qin appointed Si as alien minister.

Just at that time Zheng Guo, a man of Hann, came to cause dissension in Qin through the construction of drainage and irrigation channels.* After the work had been done he was found out. Members of the Qin royal house and important officials all told the King of Qin: 'People from the feudal states who come to serve Qin in general merely travel here to cause dissension in Qin on behalf of their own rulers. We request the complete expulsion of aliens.'* There was discussion whether Li Si should also be included among those expelled, so he submitted a memorial saying:

Your servant has heard officials discussing the expulsion of aliens, and humbly considers it to be a mistake. In earlier times, when Duke Mu was in search of public servants, he obtained You Yu from the Rong barbarians in the west and got Baili Xi from Yuan in the east. He welcomed Jian Shu from Song, and attracted Pi Bao and Gongsun Zhi from Jin. These five gentlemen were not brought up by Qin, but Duke Mu employed them, and he annexed twenty states and subsequently became overlord of the Western Rong. Making use of Shang Yang's system of law, Duke Xiao transformed the customs and usages, and the people consequently prospered and the state consequently grew rich and powerful. The common people were delighted to be employed and feudal lords became friendly and offered allegiance. He captured the Chu and Wei armies, and took 1,000 *li** of territory, so that right up to the present Qin is well governed and strong. Making use of the plans of Zhang Yi, King Hui seized the territory of Sanchuan, and in the west annexed Ba and Shu, in the north acquired the area which became the Shang province, and in the south took Hanzhong. He enveloped the nine tribes of Yi barbarians, exercised government over Yan* and Ying, and in the east occupied the crucial position of Chenggao and carved out fertile territories. Subsequently he split up the north–south alliance of the Six States and made them face west and serve Qin, and the benefit has lasted until the present. Having got hold of Fan Sui, King Zhaoxiang dismissed the Marquis of Rang and drove out Huayang. He strengthened the ruling house but put obstacles in front of private establishments. He nibbled away at the feudal states and enabled Qin to complete the imperial heritage. These four rulers all made use of the achievements of aliens. Looking at it from this point of view, surely aliens have not been ignored by Qin! Yet supposing these four rulers had rejected aliens and not admitted them, kept such public servants at a distance and not given them employment, this would have meant that the state would be without the reality of wealth and profit and that Qin would lack the reputation for strength and greatness.

At present Your Majesty has jade from the Kun Mountains* brought to him and possesses the treasure of Sui and He. From your girdle hang pearls as bright as the moon, and you wear the Taia sword. You drive horses like Xianli, put up banners adorned with green phoenixes, and set up drums made from the hide of the divine alligator. Qin does not produce one among these various treasures, so why does Your Majesty take pleasure in them? If they must be what the Qin state produces before they are acceptable, then these night-brightening jade ornaments would not embellish the court and vessels of rhinoceros-horn and ivory would not serve as your playthings, and women from Zheng and Wey would not fill the rear quarters of your palace, and fine coursers would not occupy the outer stables, the bronze and tin of Jiangnan would not be made into useful objects, and the cinnabar and blue of western Shu would not be made into paint. If the means of adorning the rear quarters of the palace and filling the lower ranks of the concubines, of giving pleasure to the heart and mind and delighting the ears and eyes, must derive from Qin before they are acceptable, then these hairpins with Yuan pearls, these ear-ornaments with long pearls attached, these silk garments from Donga, and these embroidered adornments would not come into your presence, nor would the fashionable, elegant, fascinating, and charming women of Zhao* stand at your side. Now striking earthenware jugs and banging jars, strumming the zither and smiting the thigh while singing 'Wu! Wu!' to delight the ear is truly the sound of Qin; while Zheng, Wei, Sangjian, Zhao, Yu, Wu, and Xiang are the music of different states. If you now abandon striking jugs and banging on jars and go over to the Zheng and Wei, and if you give up strumming the zither and accept the Zhao and Yu, why is it that you behave like this? What pleases our ideas we have to have in our presence. It simply suits our senses. Now when it comes to selecting men, you do not do likewise. You do not question whether they are acceptable or not and you do not discuss whether they are crooked or straight. Those who are hot from Qin are got rid of, and those who are aliens are expelled. If that is so, then what these people take seriously consists of sexual attraction, music, pearls, and jade, and what they take lightly consists of people. This is not a method with which to bestride all within the seas or control the feudal states.

Your servant has heard that when the lands are broad, grain is plentiful; when the state is large, the people are multitudinous; and when weapons are strong, men of action are valiant. So Mount Tai does not reject the soil, and therefore it can complete its size; the rivers and seas do not choose the tiny streams that flow into them, and therefore they can increase their depth; kings do not repel the masses, and therefore they are able to make their virtue continue to shine forth. Thus the earth will not have four quarters, the people will not have different countries, the four seasons will be replete and beautiful, and the ghosts and spirits will send down blessings. This is the reason why the Five Emperors and the Three Kings* were without enemies. Now in fact you are getting rid of the black-headed people so as to provide a resource for enemy countries, and you expel aliens so as to build up the strength of the feudal states. You are causing public servants from all under Heaven to hold back and not venture to turn their faces towards the west, to halt their feet and not enter Qin. This is what is called 'contributing weapons to brigands and presenting provisions to robbers'.

Now articles which are valuable although not produced by Qin are many, and public servants who wish to show their loyalty although not brought up by Qin are numerous. If you now expel aliens so as to provide a resource for enemy states and reduce your people so as to increase your foes, then you will not only be making yourself empty at home but also sowing the seeds of resentment in the feudal states. If you aim for the state to be free of dangers, this cannot be achieved.

Accordingly the King of Qin rescinded the order for the expulsion of aliens and restored Li Si to office, and ultimately he made use of his plans and stratagems. In official position he attained to the Superintendency of Trials. After more than twenty years all under Heaven was finally unified, and the sovereign was honoured as August Emperor, and he made Si chief minister. He razed the city walls in provinces and districts and melted down their weapons to demonstrate that they would not again be used. He ensured that there would be no fiefdom in Qin, even of a single foot of territory, and he did not set up his sons and younger brothers as kings* or successful ministers as feudal lords, to ensure that in future there would be none of the disasters of warfare.

In the thirty-fourth year of the First Emperor, when a banquet was arranged in the palace at Xianyang, Chief Administrator of the Scholars of Broad Learning* Zhou Qingchen and others extolled the awe-inspiring virtue of the First Emperor. Chunyu Yue, a man of Qi,* came forward and remonstrated, saying: 'Your servant has heard that the fact that the Yin and Zhou reigned for more than 1,000 years was because they enfeoffed their sons and younger brothers and successful officials to provide branches and supports for themselves. Now although Your Majesty possesses all within the seas, your sons and younger brothers are private individuals; and ultimately, if disasters such as those brought about by Tian Chang or the six ministers* occur, your subjects will have no means of support, so how will they rescue each other? That an enterprise can survive for long if it is not modelled on antiquity is not anything I have heard about. Now Qingchen and the others are also flattering you to your face so as to aggravate Your Majesty's mistakes, and it is not the case that they are loyal subjects.'

The First Emperor passed down their comments to the Chief Minister, who considered his advice to be mistaken and rejected his pronouncements. Accordingly he submitted a memorial saying:

In antiquity all under Heaven was divided and in chaos, and nobody was capable of bringing unity to the rest, and it was for this reason that the feudal lords became active together. In their utterances they all spoke of the past in order to injure the present, and they made a display of empty verbiage in order to throw the truth into confusion. People approved what they had learnt in private in order to reject what their superiors laid down. Now Your Majesty has unified and taken possession of all under Heaven. You have distinguished white from black and fixed a single focus of adulation. But those who have studied privately in fact collaborate with each other to reject the regulations laid down by law and teaching; and when they hear orders promulgated, each criticizes them in accordance with his private studies. Indoors they mentally reject them, and outdoors they make criticisms in the byways. To reject their sovereign they consider a source of fame, disagreement they regard as noble, and they encourage all the lower orders to fabricate slander. If such things are not prohibited, then above the sovereign's power will decline, and below factions will form. To prohibit this would be expedient.

Your servant requests that all who possess literature such as the *Songs*, the *Documents*, and the sayings of the hundred schools should get rid of it* without penalty. If they have not got rid of it a full thirty days after the order has reached them, they should be branded and sent to do forced labour on the walls. There should be exemption for books concerned with medicine, pharmacy, divination by tortoiseshell and milfoil,* the sowing of crops, and the planting of trees. If there are those who wish to study, they should take the law officers as their teachers.

Approving his proposals, the First Emperor collected up and got rid of the *Songs*, the *Documents*, and the sayings of the hundred schools in order to make the people stupid and ensure that in all under Heaven there should be no rejection of the present by using the past. The clarification of laws and regulations and the settling of statutes and ordinances all started with the First Emperor. He standardized documents.* Lodges to be occupied during his travels were erected, and he made extensive journeys throughout the Empire. In the following year he again made a tour of inspection and drove out the barbarians on all four sides. In all these matters Si played a powerful part.

Si's eldest son, You, was Governor of Sanchuan, and all his sons were married to Qin princesses, while his daughters were all wedded to Qin princes. When Li You, as Governor of Sanchuan, announced his return to Xianyang, Li Si arranged a banquet at home; and the more senior among all the various officials all came before him to wish him long life, and the carriages and horsemen at the gateway and in the courtyard were numbered in thousands. 'Alas!' said Li Si, sighing heavily. 'I have heard Xun Qing* say: "Things are prevented from prospering greatly." I am only a commoner from Shangcai, a black-headed person from a village lane; but the Supreme One, unaware of my decrepitude, has subsequently promoted me to this. Among those who serve at the present time nobody occupies a position superior to mine, and it may be described as the peak of wealth and honour. But when things reach their peak they decline,* and I do not at all know where I shall take off my harness.'

In the tenth month of his thirty-seventh year the First Emperor left for a tour to Kuaiji and, travelling along the coast, went north until he reached Langye. Chief Minister Si and Director of Palace Coach-houses Zhao Gao, who was concurrently in charge of the transmission of the imperial seal, were both in attendance. The First Emperor had more than twenty sons, but because the eldest son, Fusu, had frequently and frankly remonstrated with the Supreme One, he had been sent by the Supreme One to supervise the soldiers at Shang province, Meng Tian being the general in command. A younger son, Huhai, was the object of affection, and when he requested to be in attendance, the Supreme One agreed to this. None of the remaining sons was in attendance.

In the seventh month* of the same year the First Emperor reached Shaqiu. Being taken seriously ill, he ordered Zhao Gao to compose a letter to be bestowed on Prince Fusu saying: 'Leave Meng Tian in charge of the troops, take part in my funeral at Xianyang, and see to the burial.' The letter was already sealed but had not yet been handed over to the messenger when the First Emperor passed away. The letter and the imperial seal were both in Zhao Gao's place, and only the son Huhai, Chief Minister Li Si, and Zhao Gao, together with five or six favourite eunuchs, knew that the First Emperor had passed away, and none of the rest of those who were in his service knew. Li Si reflected that the Supreme One had passed away while outside the capital, leaving no real crown prince, so he kept it secret. He arranged that the First Emperor should stay inside the sleeping-carriage, and the various officials submitted business and sent up food as before, whereupon the eunuchs immediately approved all the submitted business from within the sleeping-carriage.

Taking advantage of the fact that he had retained the letter with the imperial seal which had been intended for bestowal on Fusu, Zhao Gao said to Prince Huhai: 'The Supreme One has passed away without issuing a mandate enfeoffing all his sons as kings, and he has merely bestowed a letter on his eldest son. When the eldest son arrives, he will ascend the throne as emperor; but you will be without a scrap of territory, so what are you going to do about it?'

'It is settled,' said Huhai. 'I have heard that an intelligent ruler understands his subjects and an intelligent father understands his sons. If a father departs from life and does not enfeoff all his sons, what is there that can be said?'

'It is not so,' said Zhao Gao. 'Just at this moment authority over the Empire and its salvation or destruction depend upon you, sir, and me, together with the Chief Minister, and nobody else, and I want you to bear this in mind. Moreover, making subjects of others and being made subjects by others, administering others and being administered by others—how can they be spoken about on the same day!'

'To get rid of an elder brother and set up a younger brother—this is unrighteous,' said Huhai. 'Not to accept a father's mandate but be in fear of death—this is unfilial. To depend for one's strength on the achievements of others since one's ability is weak and one's talents are shallow—this is incompetent. These three things run contrary to virtue and the Empire would not submit. My own person would probably fall into danger and the spirits of the land and grain would not accept my sacrifices.'

Gao said: 'I have heard that, when Tang and Wu* killed their rulers, all under Heaven attributed righteousness to them and they were not regarded as disloyal. When the Lord of Wey killed his father, the state of Wey recorded his virtue. Master Kong wrote about him, and he was not regarded as unfilial. In great enterprises one does not exercise trivial caution, and in making one's virtue prosper one does not refuse and shrink back. Different localities each have their own sense of propriety* and the various officials do not share the same standards of achievement. So if you turn your attention to the small and forget the great, later on harm will certainly develop; and if you are as scared as a rabbit, later on you are bound to have regrets. If one is decisive and has the courage to take action, the ghosts and spirits will steer clear of one, and later on success will be achieved. I wish you would follow this course.' Huhai sighed heavily. 'At this moment,' he said, 'the great occurrence* has not yet been revealed and the mourning rites have not yet been brought to a conclusion, so surely it would not be proper to involve the Chief Minister in this matter?' 'The time has come, the time has come!' said Zhao Gao. 'If we delay, we shall not achieve our plans. There are abundant provisions and swift horses, and the only fear is that we shall be too late.'

When Huhai had accepted Gao's argument, Gao said: 'If we do not make plans with the Chief Minister, I am afraid that the business cannot be completed, so your servant begs to make plans for this with the Chief Minister on your behalf.' Gao accordingly said to Chief Minister Si: 'The Supreme One has passed away and has bestowed on his eldest son a letter saying that he is to take part in the funeral at Xianyang and be set up as his successor. The letter has not yet been sent, but now the Supreme One has passed away, there is nobody at all who knows about it. The letter bestowed on the eldest son together with the imperial seal are both at Huhai's place,* so determining a crown prince simply depends on what Your Excellency and myself have to say. What shall we do about the matter?'

'Where did you get words which will destroy the state?' said Si. 'This is not something that a subject ought to discuss.' 'If Your Excellency were to weigh himself up,' said Gao, 'in ability who is on a par with Meng Tian? In height of achievement who is on a par with Meng Tian? In the far-sightedness and persistence of his planning who is on a par with Meng Tian? In not being resented by the Empire who is on a par with Meng Tian? In enjoying the long-standing confidence of the eldest son who is on a par with Meng Tian?' 'In all of these five things I fall short of Meng Tian,' said Si. 'How thoroughly do you reprove me!'

'Originally I was a menial from the inner departments,' said Gao, 'but fortunately I was able as a result of my work as a brush and scraper clerk* to secure advancement and enter the Qin palace. I have conducted business for more than twenty years, but I have never once come across a chief minister or successful official of Qin who has been dismissed and who has held his fief into the second generation. Ultimately they have all been executed because of it. The Emperor has more than twenty sons, all of whom you know. The eldest son is resolute and valorous. He practises good faith towards others and inspires enthusiasm in public servants. When he ascends the throne, he is bound to employ Meng Tian as chief minister, and it has become clear that you will definitely not be returning to your village cherishing your seal as marquis of the highest rank. When I received the imperial mandate to train Huhai, I made him study legal matters for several years, and I never once observed errors and omissions. He is kind, humane, sincere, and generous; he makes light of wealth but attaches weight to public servants; he is discriminating in mind and circumspect in speech; he is thorough in his performance of the rites and shows respect for public servants. Of all the sons of Qin there is not one who comes up to this one, and he should be made the successor. Having considered this, sir, settle it.'

'You should get back to your place, sir!' said Si. 'I have received our sovereign's mandate and I pay heed to the decrees of Heaven. What doubts are there to be resolved?' 'What is secure may be made dangerous and what is dangerous may be made secure,' said Gao. 'If security and danger are not settled, how may we honour the sages?'

'I am a commoner from the byways of Shangcai,' said Si, 'but through the Supreme One's favour I have been elected to be chief minister and enfeoffed as a marquis of the highest rank, and my sons and grandsons have all attained honourable positions and substantial salaries. That is why I shall take to myself commitments concerning the salvation and ruin and the security and danger of the state. How can they be ignored? The loyal subject is not doing too badly if he does not hesitate to face death, but the filial son faces danger only if he does not make an effort. Indeed it is up to each subject merely to take care of his own responsibilities. You should not repeat your words, sir, for you will cause me to give offence.'* 'Surely one hears that sages shift their ground and avoid constancy,' said Gao. 'Readily accepting change, they accord with the seasons. Seeing the branches, they are aware of the root; and observing the fingers, they see where they point. This certainly exists in natural phenomena, so where does one get constant laws?* Just at this moment the authority and destiny of the Empire depend upon Huhai, and I can get what I want out of him. Moreover, to try to control the centre from outside is termed self-deception, and to try to control superiors from an inferior position is termed rebelliousness. So when the autumn frosts descend plants and flowers die back, and when the waters stir again the myriad things become active. This is a pattern things inevitably follow. Why are you, sir, so late in seeing it?'

Si said: 'I hear that, when Jin changed its crown prince, it did not enjoy peace for three generations; when Huan of Qi struggled with his brother for the throne, his body was desecrated after his death; and when Zhou killed his relative and did not pay heed to those who remonstrated with him, the state became a wasteland and subsequently the altars of the land and grain were imperilled. Since these three events* were in defiance of Heaven, the ancestral temples would not accept the sacrifices. I should indeed be just like those people. Surely he is not worth plotting for!'

'When superior and inferior are in harmony together,' said Gao, 'they may long survive; when the centre and the periphery are as one, then matters will have no ins and outs. If you, sir, listen to your servant's plans, then you will long retain your fief, and the title will continue for generation after generation, and you will certainly possess the longevity of a lofty pine and the wisdom of a Kong or a Mo.* Now if you let this opportunity slip and do not join in, disasters will befall your sons and grandsons, sufficient to make your heart turn cold. Those who are skilful make use of disaster to produce good fortune, so what position do you adopt in this?'

Si thereupon looked up to Heaven and groaned. Shedding tears, he sighed deeply and said: 'Alas! I encounter a time of trouble on my own, and since I am incapable of facing death because of it, to what am I to entrust my fate?' Thereupon Si did in fact pay heed to Gao. Gao accordingly reported to Huhai: 'Your servant requests to receive the Crown Prince's illustrious decree and report it to the Chief Minister, for Chief Minister Si will not presume not to accept your commands.'

Thereupon they did in fact plot together and pretended to have received a mandate from the First Emperor to the Chief Minister that his son Huhai was to be set up as crown prince. The letter for bestowal on the eldest son, Fusu, was rewritten as follows: 'In Our travels throughout the Empire We pray and sacrifice to the various spirits of the famous mountains in order to prolong Our allotted span.* Now for more than a decade Fusu, in association with General Meng Tian,* has been in command of an army of several hundred thousand for the purpose of garrisoning the frontier, but he has not been able to be received into our presence, having made an advance. Many officers and soldiers have been wasted without a scrap of success, but he has actually submitted several frankly worded letters libelling what We are doing. Consequently he has not obtained relief from this responsibility so as to return as crown prince, and day and night he has felt resentful. Being a son but not behaving in a filial manner, Fusu is to be presented with a sword so that he may dispatch himself. Being stationed outside the capital with Fusu, General Tian behaved incorrectly, for he ought to have been aware of his plotting. Being a subject but showing disloyalty, he is to be presented with death and his troops are to be handed over to Assistant General Wang Li.' His letter was sealed with the imperial seal, and a dependant of Huhai was dispatched to take the letter and present it to Fusu in Shang province.

When the messenger arrived, he produced the letter. Fusu wept and entered his inner quarters, intending to kill himself. But Meng Tian stopped Fusu. 'His Majesty was in quarters outside the capital,' he said, 'and had not yet set up a crown prince. He appointed your servant to take command of a host of 300,000 to guard the frontier, and Your Highness was made supervisor, and these are weighty responsibilities of empire. Now if one kills oneself when a single messenger comes, how does one know that he is not being deceitful? Put in a request for confirmation; and if having done so you die afterwards, that will not be too late.' The messenger urged them repeatedly and, since he was a man of humane qualities, Fusu said to Meng Tian: 'If he bestows death upon me although he is my father, how can he nevertheless be asked for confirmation?' And so he killed himself. Meng Tian refused to die, so the messenger at once handed him over to the law officers and he was imprisoned at Yangzhou.

When the messenger returned and reported, Huhai, Si, and Gao were highly delighted. When they reached Xianyang, they announced the mourning, and the Crown Prince was set up as

Second Generation Emperor. Zhao Gao was appointed Director
of Palace Gentlemen. He was constantly in attendance and in control of whatever happened at the palace.

The Second Generation Emperor was taking his ease, so he
summoned Gao to plan business with him. 'As for the span of
time during which a man lives and dwells in the world,' he said,
'it is just like driving six fine horses past a crack. Now that I have
taken charge of the Empire, I wish to experience to the full those
things which my ears and eyes are fond of and thoroughly enjoy
what my heart and will delight in, in such a way as to bring peace
to the ancestral temples and delight to the myriad clans, to possess the Empire for a long time, and to complete my full span of
years. Is a way of achieving this possible?'

'This,' said Gao, 'is what the talented sovereign is capable of
achieving, but what the stupid and disorganized sovereign is
debarred from. Your servant begs to talk about this and, not pre-
suming to evade the punishment of the axe, he would like Your
Majesty to let his thoughts dwell for a little on this. As far as the
Shaqiu plot is concerned, the princes and important ministers all
feel dubious about it; and furthermore the princes are all elder
brothers of the Emperor, and the important officials are also people
who were put into office by the previous Emperor. At present
Your Majesty has only just been set on the throne, so these men
will be discontented in their allegiance to you and none of them
will be subservient. I fear that they will make a rebellion. Moreover,
although Meng Tian is dead,* Meng Yi is stationed outside the capital in command of troops; and so your servant goes in fear and
trembling, his worry being simply that you will not complete your
span. So on top of all this how can Your Majesty indulge in these
delights?'

'What shall I do about it?' said the Second Generation Emperor.
'Make the law severe and the punishments harsh,' said Zhao Gao,
'and command that those who have committed crimes should
involve others* in their trials and punishments, going so far as the
arrest and extermination of the whole clan. Wipe out the important officials and keep your own flesh and blood at a distance; enrich
the poor and honour the lowly. Get rid of the erstwhile officials of

the previous Emperor completely and, having replaced them with ones whom Your Majesty intimately trusts, keep them close to you. If this is done, then the hidden charisma of the ruler will come to belong to Your Majesty, sources of harm will be eradicated, and treacherous plotting will be prevented, and none of the whole band of officials will not be the recipient of your beneficence or the object of your generosity. As far as Your Majesty is concerned, you will rest on a high pillow, giving full scope to your desires and favour to your pleasures. In your planning nothing should deviate from this.'

Second Generation accepted Gao's arguments, and so he reformed the laws and statutes. Thereupon if one of the officials or princesses committed a crime, he was immediately handed over to Gao with orders for him to be tried. He put to death the important official Meng Yi and others, and twelve princes were executed in the market-place at Xianyang, and ten princes were drawn and quartered at Du. Their property was taken in by the district offices, and countless people were tried for being implicated with them.

Prince Gao wished to flee, but he was afraid his clan would be arrested and exterminated, so he submitted a letter saying: 'When the previous Emperor enjoyed good health, upon entering the palace your servant had food bestowed upon him, and upon leaving he rode in a carriage. Clothing from the imperial storehouse your servant had bestowed upon him, and valuable horses from the palace stables your servant had bestowed upon him. Your servant ought to have accompanied him in death but he could not. As a son he is unfilial and as a subject disloyal. The disloyal have no reputation with which to take their stand in their generation, so your servant requests to accompany him in death, and would like to be buried at the foot of Mount Li.* May the Supreme One have the kindness to take pity on him.' When the letter was submitted Huhai was highly delighted. He summoned Zhao Gao and showed it to him, saying: 'This can be called getting a move on, can it not?' 'Your subjects ought to die of grief and not waste time,' said Zhao Gao, 'and then what rebellions would they succeed in plotting!' Huhai approved his letter and bestowed 100,000 copper coins for the burial.

The laws and punishments day by day became increasingly harsh, and each one of the ministers felt himself to be in danger, and there were many who wished to rebel. He also built the Epang palace and constructed direct routes and express routes, so that taxation became all the more burdensome and forced labour for service on the frontier was interminable. Thereupon the frontier soldiers Chen Sheng, Wu Guang, and others did in fact make a revolt. They rose up in the area east of the mountains:* local heroes set each other up and they arranged for themselves to be treated as marquises and kings and rebelled against the Qin. Their soldiers got as far as Hongmen before being repelled.

On several occasions Li Si wanted to make a request for the opportunity to remonstrate, but Second Generation would not give permission. Instead he reproachfully questioned Li Si as follows: 'I have been the recipient of confidential advice, including something which I heard from Master Han,* who told me that when Yao possessed all under Heaven, his reception hall was only 3 feet off the ground,* his oaken rafters were not cut to size, and his thatch of reeds was not trimmed. Even a travellers' lodging is not more austere than this. In winter days he wore deerskins and in summer days clothing made of the *ge* plant. Coarse grain was what he ate, and the *li* and *huo* plants he used for broth. He ate and drank from earthenware bowls. Even a gatekeeper's nourishment is not more frugal than this. Yu* forced a passage through Longmen and made a way through Daxia. He separated off the nine rivers and created nine dykes to divert them. He released the stagnant waters and made them go into the sea, so that his thighs and shins were worn smooth and hairless, his hands and feet were covered in calluses, and his face and eyes were blackened. Subsequently he died away from home and was buried at Kuaiji. The labours of a slave are not more arduous than this.

'This being the case then, the one whom people honour in that he possesses the Empire surely does not wish to make his body suffer or weary his spirit, with his person occupying a travellers' lodging, his mouth consuming the fare of a gatekeeper, and his hands getting to grips with the work of a slave. This is what a degenerate person puts his efforts into, and not what a man of quality strives at. When such a man of quality has possession of the Empire, he concentrates on making use of the Empire just to suit himself, and this is the reason why he is honoured for possessing the Empire. Now the so-called man of quality must be capable of pacifying the Empire and governing its myriad peoples. Now if he is unable to profit even his own person, how will he be able to govern the Empire? Therefore I want to be indulgent towards my impulses and give wide scope to my desires, and to avoid harm while I long enjoy the fruits of Empire. What shall I do to achieve this?'

Li Si's son You was Governor of Sanchuan, and when the bandit hordes of Wu Guang and the others came west and seized territory, he could not prevent them passing through. When Zhang Han had smashed and driven out the soldiers of Guang and the others, emissaries had repeatedly investigated Sanchuan and associated areas, and they blamed Si on the ground that there was a question how it was that, although he occupied one of the three highest offices of state, he enabled bandits to behave like this. Li Si was terrified and, regarding the preservation of his rank and salary as important but not knowing what to come up with, he servilely accepted Second Generation's ideas and, wishing to seek forbearance, he replied with a memorial which stated:

The sovereign of quality is one who must be capable of developing a complete system for practising the techniques of supervision and allocating responsibility.* When he supervises them and allocates responsibility to them, subjects do not dare not to exhaust their abilities so as to devote their lives to their sovereign. Thus when the distinction between subject and sovereign is fixed and the duties of superior and inferior are made clear, then nobody in the Empire, whether man of quality or not, will dare not to make every effort to fulfil his duties in order to devote his life to his ruler. That is why the sovereign alone governs in the Empire and yet there are none whom he governs. Since he will become capable of thoroughly enjoying the extremes of pleasure, should not a sovereign of quality and intelligence look into this?

So when Master Shen* said, 'Possessing all under Heaven and not acting without constraint is called treating all under Heaven as shackles,' he did so for no other reason than this: if one cannot supervise and allocate responsibility, but instead toils with one's body for all the people under

Heaven, just as Yao and Yu did, it is therefore called 'shackles'. Now if one cannot cultivate the intelligent techniques of Shen and Han and practise the system of supervision and allocating responsibility, concentrating on making use of the Empire to suit oneself; but if one merely devotes oneself to making one's body suffer and wearying one's spirit, so as to use one's body to devote oneself to the common people, then this is to be a menial of the black-headed ones, and not to be one who treats the Empire as his flock. How is such a person worth honouring? For if you make others devote their lives to yourself, then you yourself are honoured and the others are lowly; but if you make yourself devote your life to others, then you yourself are lowly and the others are honoured. That is why those who devote their lives to others are lowly and those to whom others devote their lives are honoured, and from antiquity until the present it has never been otherwise. In all cases the reason why ancients honoured men of quality was because of their honoured position, and the reason why they hated men of no quality was because of their low rank. But Yao and Yu were ones who used their bodies to devote themselves to all under Heaven; and if one venerates them as a consequence of this, then one is surely losing the attitude of mind on account of which one venerates men of quality, and this may be described as great self-deception. Is it not therefore reasonable to describe it as 'shackles'? It is the error of not being capable of supervision and allocating responsibility.

So why is it that Master Han said: 'The indulgent mother has a prodigal son but the strict family has no recalcitrant slaves'? It is because the capacity to inflict punishments on them is unavoidable. Therefore the laws of Lord Shang punished people who threw ashes out on the road. Now throwing ashes out is a trivial crime, but suffering the punishment of the law is a heavy penalty. Thus only the intelligent ruler is regarded as capable of exercising thorough supervision of unimportant offences. If the supervision is thorough even when the offence is unimportant, how much more should it be so when there is a serious offence? That is why the people do not dare to transgress. Therefore Master Han said: 'A tiny piece of cloth the ordinary person will not pass over, but 2,000 taels of molten metal Robber Zhi will not snatch.' This is not because the ordinary person's mind exaggerates the value of a tiny piece of cloth or because Robber Zhi's desires are weak. Moreover one does not consider that the conduct of Robber Zhi undervalues a weight of 2,000 taels. If he snatches, this is bound to result in punishment for the hand, so Robber Zhi does not snatch the 2,000 taels; but if a penalty did not automatically come into effect, the ordinary person would not pass over a tiny piece of cloth. That is why a city wall 50 feet high even Lou Ji* does not lightly cross, but although the height of Mount Tai is 800 feet lame ewes are tended on its summit. Now if even Lou Ji finds a 50 foot barrier difficult, surely lame ewes do not find a height of 800 feet easy. The situations are different as regards steepness.

As for the reason why the intelligent sovereign or the sage-king can long occupy a venerated position and continuously wield the weightiest authority, so as to monopolize the profits of the Empire, it is not the case that he possesses any different method: he is capable of taking decisions on his own and exercising supervision and allocating responsibility in a discriminating manner. He makes severe punishments follow automatically, and that is the reason why the Empire does not dare to transgress. If one does not concern oneself with how to prevent transgression, but acts in the way the indulgent mother treats the prodigal son, then surely one has not looked into the discussions of the sages. Now if one cannot practise the techniques of the sage, then one is dismissed as a menial of the Empire, and what is there to do? Should one not be the object of pity!

Moreover if men who are frugal, economical, humane, and righteous* take their positions in court, then reckless and dissolute pleasures are stopped. If officials who give remonstrating advice and discuss principles take their leisure at your side, then dissolute intentions will be thwarted. If the conduct of ardent men of action who will die for their principles is displayed to the age, then wanton pleasures are eradicated. Therefore the intelligent sovereign is capable of keeping out these three sorts of people, so that he alone takes a firm grip on the technique of ruling in order to control subjects who pay heed and accept his lead. And if he cultivates his intelligent laws, for this reason he himself will be venerated and his authority will be weighty. In all cases sovereigns of quality are bound to be able to be at odds with their generation and to mould its customs so as to get rid of what they hate and establish what they desire; and that is the reason why, while they are alive, they possess an authority which is venerated and weighty, and when they die they have posthumous titles redolent of quality and intelligence. So since the intelligent ruler takes decisions on his own, authority consequently does not lie in the hands of his subordinates. Only in these circumstances can he obliterate the path of humaneness and righteousness, cover the mouths of garrulous speakers, frustrate the activities of ardent men of action, put up a barrier to wisdom and a shroud over intelligence, so that within the palace he sees and listens on his own. Consequently, when away from the palace, he cannot be overthrown by the activities of the humane and the righteous and of ardent men of action; and when he is inside the palace, he cannot be grabbed by the arguments of those who advise remonstratingly or wrangle angrily. Therefore he is able openly and independently to activate a licentious heart, and nobody dares to oppose him. Only after he has behaved like this can he be said to be capable of understanding the techniques of Shen and Han and of cultivating the law of Lord Shang. I have never heard of all under Heaven being in chaos if this law is cultivated and these techniques understood. That is why it is said that 'The kingly way is to handle things easily by imposing restraint.'

Only the intelligent sovereign seems capable of practising this. If he behaves like this, then he may be said to be practising supervision and allocating responsibility. If he really and truly does so, then the subjects are without depravity; and if the subjects are without depravity, then all under Heaven is at peace; if all under Heaven is at peace, then the sovereign's severity is venerated; if the sovereign's severity is venerated, then the supervision and the allocation of responsibility become automatic; if the supervision and the allocation of responsibility become automatic, then what is sought is obtained; if what is sought is obtained, then the nation becomes rich; if the nation becomes rich, then the ruler's pleasures are abundant. So when the techniques of supervision and allocating responsibility are established, then everything which is desired is obtained. If all the officials and the common people are not granted a respite from their mistakes, then what rebellion is it that they will venture to plot? In such circumstances the Emperor's way is made perfect, and he may be said to be capable of understanding the techniques which govern the relationship between ruler and subject. If even a Shen or a Han came to life again, they could not make any addition.

When the memorial was presented, Second Generation was pleased. Thereupon the practice of supervision and allocating responsibility became increasingly severe, and those who were thorough in their taxation of the people were regarded as intelligent officers. Second Generation said: 'If they perform like this then they may be said to be capable of practising supervision and allocating responsibility.' People who had suffered punishment comprised half of those seen on the roads, and day by day corpses formed heaps in the market-place. Those who killed a multitude of people were regarded as loyal subjects. Second Generation said: 'If they perform like this then they may be said to be capable of practising supervision and allocating responsibility.'

Before this, when Zhao Gao became Director of Palace Gentlemen, the crowd of those whom he had killed or paid back over private grievances was numerous, so he was afraid that, when the important officials came to court to present business, they would vilify him. So he addressed Second Generation as follows: 'The reason why the Son of Heaven is honoured is because only his voice is heard, and none of his subjects can see his face. That is why he refers to himself as "the mysterious one".* Moreover Your Majesty has a rich store of springs and autumns to come, and is bound not yet to be fully conversant with all matters. At present when you sit at court and there is something inappropriate in the criticisms or recommendations made, you reveal your shortcomings to the important officials, and that is not how to demonstrate spirit-like intelligence to the Empire. Moreover if Your Majesty were to hold yourself in an attitude of deep reverence within the forbidden precincts and left it to your servant together with those palace attendants who are experienced in the law to deal with business, then when business comes in, there will be a procedure for considering it. In such circumstances the important officials will not venture to submit questionable matters, and the Empire will acclaim a sage ruler.' Second Generation adopted his plan, and accordingly did not sit at court and receive important officials, but stayed within the forbidden precincts. Zhao Gao was in constant attendance and was in control of whatever happened in the palace, and the business was all decided by Zhao Gao.

Zhao Gao heard that Li Si had made remarks about this, so he went to see the Chief Minister and said: 'The bandit hordes in the area east of the pass have grown numerous, yet at the present time the Supreme One impatiently sends an increasing number of forced labourers to build the Epang palace, and he collects dogs and horses and useless objects. I wish to remonstrate but am regarded as lowly in position. This is really a job for Your Excellency. Why do you not remonstrate, sir?' 'To be sure,' said Li Si, 'I intended to mention this a long time ago. At the present time the Supreme One does not sit at court but stays in the depths of the palace and, although I have something to say, it cannot be passed on, and when I wish to have audience, he has no time to spare.'

'If you are really capable of remonstrating with him,' said Zhao Gao, 'I shall make a request on your behalf, sir, that you may wait for the time when the Supreme One has the leisure to speak with you.'

Thereupon Zhao Gao waited until the precise moment when Second Generation was feasting and enjoying himself, with women in his presence, when he sent someone to report to the Chief Minister: 'The Supreme One is at this moment free, and he can have business submitted to him.' The Chief Minister went to the palace gate and sent in an announcement of his visit, and the same thing happened three times. 'I always have a lot of free days, but the Chief Minister does not come,' said Second Generation furiously. 'Yet just at the precise moment when I am feasting and enjoying privacy, the Chief Minister immediately comes to request that we talk business. Surely the Chief Minister thinks I am too young, and that is why he puts pressure on me?'

'If he behaves like this, he has become a menace,' said Zhao Gao, seizing the opportunity. 'That plot at Shaqiu—the Chief Minister was a party to it. Now Your Majesty has been set up as emperor, but the Chief Minister's honours do not increase, so at the back of his mind there is surely the hope that he may annex territory and reign as a king. Moreover since Your Majesty did not question your servant, he did not presume to speak. But the Chief Minister's eldest son, Li You, is Governor of Sanchuan, and the Chu brigands, Chen Sheng and the rest, are all offspring of the districts adjacent to the Chief Minister's. For this reason the Chu brigands are acting openly, and when they passed through Sanchuan, the Governor refused to strike. I hear that documents pass backwards and forwards between them, but since I have not yet got evidence of this, I have therefore not yet ventured to report it. Moreover the Chief Minister resides outside the palace, and his authority is weightier than that of Your Majesty.' Second Generation thought that it was true. He wished that the Chief Minister be investigated, but was afraid that he did not have evidence, so he sent someone to bring forward proof against the Governor of Sanchuan on a charge of being in collusion with the brigands. Li Si heard about this.

At this time Second Generation was at Ganquan, where displays of all-in wrestling* and theatricals had just been put on. Since Li Si could not obtain audience, he consequently submitted a letter mentioning Zhao Gao's shortcomings, saying: 'Your servant has heard that when a subject undermines his ruler's confidence, it always imperils the state; and when a concubine makes her master distrust her, it always endangers the family. Now there is an important official who usurps from Your Majesty the imposition of both profit and harm. He is on a par with Your Majesty, and this is very inexpedient. In former times when Minister of Works Zihan became chief minister to Song, he personally administered punishments, and did so in an authoritative manner, and then a year later he forced his ruler into exile. When Tian Chang was in the service of Duke Jian, his rank was unrivalled in the state, and the wealth of his private household was equal to that of the ducal household. By making a show of kindness and distributing bounties, he won over the common people below and the various officials above. He worked in secret to take over the state of Qi: having killed Zai Yu at court, he then assassinated Duke Jian in the audience chamber, and subsequently took possession of the state of Qi. These facts are what all under Heaven are plainly aware of. Now Gao has a depraved and unbridled ambition, and his conduct is dangerous and subversive, and he behaves like Zihan when he was chief minister to Song. The wealth of his private household is like the Tian family's in relation to Qi. He practises a combination of the seditious methods of Tian Chang and Zihan so as to oust the awe-inspiring good faith of Your Majesty, and his ambition is like that of Han Yi* when he became chief minister of An of Hann. If Your Majesty does not take precautions, your servant fears that he will make a rebellion.'

'What!' exclaimed Second Generation.* 'This Gao has long been an eunuch, but he has not given scope to ambition for the sake of his own security, and he has not changed his mind because of danger. By keeping his behaviour clean and practising his skills, he has enabled himself to attain this position. Through loyalty he has obtained access to me, and through good faith he has preserved his position. We* truly consider him a man of quality, so why do you, sir, doubt him? Moreover We were young when We lost Our father, and there was nothing which We understood and We were not practised in governing the people; whereas you, sir, had also grown old, and the fear was that you had become cut off from the Empire. If We had not enlisted the help of Lord Zhao, to whom ought We to have entrusted responsibility? Moreover Lord Zhao is a man who is strong and incorruptible in spirit. Below he understands the nature of men, and above he is capable of suiting Ourselves. You should not doubt him, sir.'

'It is not true,' said Li Si. 'This Gao was originally a man of lowly birth. He lacks understanding of principle and his greedy desires can never be satisfied. He does not rest in his search for profit and his rank and power are second only to those of his sovereign. Since his pursuit of what he desires is unremitting, I therefore say that he is a menace.' Since Second Generation already had confidence in Zhao Gao and was afraid that Li Si would kill him, he therefore privately informed Zhao Gao. 'I am the only one the Chief Minister is worried about,' said Gao. 'When I am dead, the Chief Minister immediately intends to do what Tian Chang did.' Thereupon Second Generation said: 'Li Si is to be handed over to the Director of Palace Gentlemen.'

Zhao Gao brought Li Si to trial. Li Si was seized and bound and, while he was staying in prison, he looked up to Heaven and sighed. 'Alas, how tragic!' he said. 'How can an unprincipled ruler be planned for? In former times Jie killed Guan Longfeng,* Zhou killed Prince Bi Gan, and Fucha King of Wu killed Wu Zixu. These three ministers were surely not disloyal, but nevertheless they did not escape from death. When they died, the ones to whom they had been loyal were in the wrong. If my wisdom is not up to that of the three gentlemen but Second Generation's lack of principle surpasses that of Jie, Zhou, and Fucha, it is reasonable that I should die through loyalty.

'Moreover Second Generation's rule will surely lead to chaos. In the past he wiped out his brothers to set himself on the throne. He killed loyal officials and gave honours to base men. He taxed the Empire to construct Epang palace. It is not that I did not remonstrate, but that he did not listen to me. In all cases the sage-kings of old had regulations for their eating and drinking, had a definite number of carriages and utensils, and had a limit to their palaces and mansions; and when they issued orders for building work, what added to expenditure and contained no increase in the people's benefit was forbidden, and therefore they were able to govern and remain secure for a long time. Now in activating charges of sedition against his brothers, he has not concerned himself with whether they are guilty; and in ill-treating and killing off loyal officials, he has not thought of their misfortunes. He builds palaces and mansions on a grand scale and heavily taxes the Empire, but does not begrudge the waste of money involved in this. Because these three things have been done, the Empire does not pay heed to him. Now the rebels have already gained possession of half of the Empire, but his mind has still not yet woken up. Instead he makes Zhao Gao his assistant. We shall certainly see bandits reaching Xianyang and wild deer at large in the audience chamber.'

Thereupon Second Generation did actually make Gao deal with the Chief Minister's case and try his offence. He charged Si with a case of plotting rebellion together with his son You, and arrested the kinsmen and dependants of them both. When he tried Si, Zhao Gao had him flogged more than 1,000 times and, since he could not bear the pain, he made a false confession. As for the reason why Si did not die,* he took it upon himself to give an explanation of his activities, assuming that, since he had achievements to his credit and truly had no intention of rebelling, he would have the good fortune to be able to submit a letter to the Supreme One setting out an account of himself, and would also have the good fortune that Second Generation would wake up and pardon him. So Li Si submitted a letter from gaol saying:

'Your servant has become chief minister and has governed the people for more than thirty years. He has extended the narrow confines of the territory of Qin. In the time of the previous King, Qin territory did not exceed 1,000 *li*, and the soldiers amounted to a few hundred thousand. Deploying all his meagre talents, your servant paid careful attention to the laws and commands he received. He secretly dispatched plotters, providing them with gold and jade and making them travel about and advise feudal lords.

He secretly prepared armour and weapons while making a display of the teachings of government. He gave office to pugnacious men of action and gave honours to successful officials, lavishly improving their ranks and salaries. And so in the end by these means Hann was coerced, Wei was weakened, Yan and Zhao were smashed, Qi and Chu were flattened, and finally the Six States were annexed, their kings were made captive, and Qin was set up as Son of Heaven. Crime number one.

'Although the territory was not unextensive, in the north the Hu and Mo were driven back and in the south the various Yue were made to submit, in order to demonstrate the strength of Qin. Crime number two. Important officials were honoured and their salaries and positions lavishly improved, in order to secure their allegiance. Crime number three. Altars of the land and grain were established, and the ancestral temples were repaired in order to make the sovereign's qualities shine forth. Crime number four. Measures of capacity, weight, and size, together with written documents, were standardized and published throughout the Empire to implant the fame of Qin. Crime number five. Express roads were built and tours of inspection were promoted in order to demonstrate that the sovereign had fulfilled his ambition. Crime number six. Punishments were relaxed and taxation was reduced in order to ensure that the sovereign would win the hearts and minds of the multitude, so that the myriad people would support their sovereign and not forget him even in death. Crime number seven. The crimes of one who behaved as a subject as I have done would certainly have merited death long since, and yet by the Supreme One's favour I have used to the full my ability and strength and thus have managed to survive to the present. I wish Your Majesty would look into this.' When the letter was submitted, Zhao Gao sent a clerk to reject it and not present it, saying: 'How can a prisoner submit a letter?'

Zhao Gao then sent a dozen or so of his dependants masquerading as imperial secretaries, ushers, and palace attendants to go in turn and renew Li Si's interrogation. When Si again replied in accordance with the truth of the matter, he immediately made people give him another flogging. Later on, when Second Generation sent people to examine Li Si, Si thought it would be just as before, so he did not at all dare to plead further, but just confessed. When it was reported to the Supreme One that the matter had reached an appropriate conclusion, Second Generation was delighted. 'But for Lord Zhao,' he said, 'I was close to being sold by the Chief Minister.' By the time that the person who had been sent by Second Generation to investigate the Governor of Sanchuan had arrived, Xiang Liang* had already attacked and killed him. When the envoy came back, it so happened that the Chief Minister had already been handed over to the law officers, and Zhao Gao dishonestly fabricated a charge of sedition against him with regard to all these matters.

In the seventh month of the second year of Second Generation the five punishments* were prepared for Si, and he was condemned to be cut in two at the waist in the market-place at Xianyang. As Si left the prison, he and his middle son were supporting each other when, turning to him, he said: 'I would like to go with you again and take our tawny dog out through the eastern gate of Shangcai to chase the cunning hare, but how could that be done!' Then father and son wept over each other, and eventually the kindred were exterminated to the third degree.*

Li Si having died, Second Generation appointed Zhao Gao to be Chief Minister from the Palace,* and business, no matter whether important or unimportant, was immediately decided by Gao. Gao was himself aware that his authority was weighty, so he presented a deer, but called it a horse.* 'This is really a deer, is it not?' Second Generation asked his courtiers, but the courtiers all said: 'It is a horse.' Second Generation was astonished and thought that he was suffering from delusions, so he summoned the Grand Diviner and ordered him to practise his arts on this matter. The Grand Diviner said: 'When Your Majesty takes part in the seasonal worship at the bounds in spring and autumn and when you make offerings to ghosts and spirits in the ancestral temples, you have been impure in your fasting, and so it has come to this. You should depend on making your virtue abundant and your abstinence clear.' So he thereupon entered Shanglin* to fast. But every day he went out hunting and shooting and, when a traveller came into Shanglin, Second Generation personally shot and killed him.

Zhao Gao instructed his son-in-law* Yan Yue, Governor of Xianyang, to prosecute whoever it might be who had murdered someone and was at large in Shanglin. Gao then remonstrated with Second Generation. 'The Son of Heaven has murdered an innocent man without cause,' he said, 'and this is forbidden by God, so the ghosts and spirits will not accept sacrifices. Heaven will send down calamities, so you ought to take yourself a long way away from the palace in order to expiate this.' So Second Generation went away and took up residence at the palace of Wangyi.

When he had been staying there for three days, Zhao Gao counterfeited an imperial edict instructing all the members of the guard to face towards the inner palace carrying weapons but wearing plain clothes. Then he went in and reported to Second Generation: 'A horde of bandit-soldiers from east of the mountains has arrived in force.' When Second Generation climbed an observation tower and saw them, he was terrified; and Gao immediately took the opportunity to force him to kill himself. He took the imperial seal and hung it from his own belt, but none of the officials who were present would accept his leadership; and by the time he went up to the audience chamber the building itself several times seemed on the point of collapsing. Since he himself had become aware that Heaven would not grant him the throne, and the various officials would not agree to it, he then summoned the First Emperor's younger brother* and conferred on him the imperial seal.

When Ziying ascended the throne, he was worried about Gao, so he pleaded illness and did not attend to business. Together with the eunuch Han Tan and his sons, he plotted to kill him. When Gao submitted an announcement of his visit to enquire after his health, he consequently summoned him in, and ordered Han Tan to stab him to death. His kindred were exterminated to the third degree.

Three months after Ziying was set on the throne, soldiers of the Governor of Pei entered via the Wu Pass,* and when they reached Xianyang, the various ministers and officials all rebelled and did not offer any resistance. Ziying, accompanied by his wife and children, tied a rope round his neck and surrendered close to Zhidao. The Governor of Pei consequently handed him over to the law officers and, when King Xiang arrived, he was beheaded. Subsequently the Empire was lost as a result of this.

The Grand Historiographer says: 'From the village lanes Li Si went through the feudal states before entering the service of Qin, and consequently exploited their defects to support the First Emperor, and ultimately brought to completion the imperial heritage. Si became one of the three highest ministers, which may be described as honourable employment. Si understood the aims of the Six Classics* but he did not concern himself with enlightened government so as to repair the sovereign's defects. Although he held on to the most substantial of ranks and salaries, he gave his assent to reckless associations. He made his authority severe and made the punishments harsh. Heeding Gao's depraved arguments, he got rid of the legitimate heir and set up the son of a concubine. When the feudal states had already rebelled, Si consequently wished to remonstrate, but surely that was dealing with the branch rather than the root? Men all take it that Si suffered the five punishments and died through his extreme loyalty, but if one examines the root of the matter, it is in fact different from the common judgement. If it were not so, Si's achievement would be on a par with those of Zhou and Shao.'*

4

THE BUILDER OF THE GREAT WALL

There now follows a short biography of Meng Tian (chapter 88), who built the Great Wall of China.

As for Meng Tian, his forebears were men of Qi. Tian's paternal grandfather, Meng Ao, came from Qi to serve King Zhaoxiang of Qin, and attained the office of senior minister. In the first year of King Zhuangxiang of Qin, Meng Ao became general of Qin, made an assault on Hann and took Chenggao and Xingyang, and established the Sanchuan province. In the second year Meng Ao attacked Zhao and took thirty-seven cities. In the third year of the First Emperor, Meng Ao attacked Hann and took thirteen cities. In the fifth year Meng Ao attacked Wei, took twenty cities, and established Dong province. In the seventh year of the First Emperor, Meng Ao died. Ao's son was called Wu and Wu's son was called Tian. Tian at one time kept legal records and was in charge of the relevant literature. In the twenty-third year of the First Emperor, Meng Wu became an assistant general of Qin and, together with Wang Jian, made an attack on Chu and inflicted a major defeat upon it and killed Xiang Yan. In the twenty-fourth year Meng Wu attacked Chu and took the King of Chu prisoner. Meng Tian's younger brother was Meng Yi.

In the twenty-sixth year of the First Emperor, Meng Tian was able to become a general of Qin on account of the long-term service given by his family. He attacked Qi and inflicted a major defeat upon it, and was appointed Prefect of the Capital. When Qin had unified all under Heaven, Meng Tian was consequently given command of a host of 300,000 to go north and drive out the Rong and Di barbarians and take over the territory to the south of the Yellow River.* He built the Great Wall, taking advantage of the lie of the land and making use of the passes. It started from Lintao and went as far as Liaodong, extending more than 10,000 *li*. Crossing the

Yellow River, it followed the Yang Mountains and wriggled northwards. His army was exposed to the elements in the field for more than ten years when they were stationed in Shang province, and at this time Meng Tian filled the Xiongnu with terror.

The First Emperor held the Meng family in the highest esteem. Having confidence in them and so entrusting them with responsibility, he regarded them as men of quality. He allowed Meng Yi to be on terms of close intimacy, and he reached the position of senior minister. When he went out, he took him with him in his carriage, and within the palace he was constantly in the imperial presence. Tian was given responsibility for matters outside the capital, but Yi was constantly made to take part in internal planning. They were reputed to be loyal and trustworthy, so that none even of the generals or leading ministers dared to take issue with them in these matters.

Zhao Gao* was a distant connection of the various Zhaos. He had several brothers, and all of them were born in the hidden part of the palace. His mother had been condemned to death, and her descendants were to be of low station for generations to come. When the King of Qin* heard that Zhao Gao was forceful and well acquainted with the law, he promoted him and made him Director of Palace Coach-houses. Thereupon Gao privately served Prince Huhai and gave him instruction in judicial decisions. When Zhao Gao committed a major crime, the King of Qin ordered Meng Yi to try him at law. Yi did not dare to show partiality, so he condemned Gao to death and removed him from the register of officials, but because of Gao's estimable performance in the conduct of affairs, the Emperor pardoned him and restored his office and rank.

The First Emperor intended to travel throughout the Empire and go via Jiuyuan directly to Ganquan, so he made Meng Tian open up a road from Jiuyuan straight to Ganquan, hollowing out mountains and filling in valleys for 1,800 *li*. The road had not yet been completed when the First Emperor in the winter of the thirty-seventh year went forth on his journey and travelled to Kuaiji. Going along the sea coast, he went north to Langye. When he fell ill on the way, he made Meng Yi return to offer prayers to the mountains and streams. He had not yet got back when the First Emperor passed away on reaching Shaqiu. It was kept a secret, and none of the officials knew. At this time Chief Minister Li Si, Prince Huhai, and Director of Palace Coach-houses Zhao Gao were in constant attendance. Gao had regularly obtained favours from Huhai and wanted him to be set on the throne. He was also resentful that when Meng Yi had tried him at law he had not been in favour of letting him off. Consequently he felt like doing him harm, and so he secretly plotted together with Chief Minister Li Si and Prince Huhai to establish Huhai as crown prince. When the Crown Prince had been established, messengers were sent to bestow death on Prince Fusu and Meng Tian because of their alleged crimes. Even after Fusu was dead, Meng Tian felt suspicious and requested confirmation of it. The messengers handed Meng Tian over to the law officers and replaced him.

The messengers returned and made their report, and when Huhai heard that Fusu was dead he intended to free Meng Tian. But Zhao Gao, fearing that the Meng family would again be treated with honour and be employed on affairs, felt resentful about this.

So when Meng Yi got back, Zhao Gao, making his plans on the pretext of loyalty towards Huhai, intended on this account to wipe out the Meng family. 'Your servant hears that the previous Emperor had long intended to promote a man of quality and set up a crown prince,' he therefore said, 'but Meng Yi had remonstrated and said that this would be improper. But if he was aware that you were a man of quality and yet insisted that you should not be set up, this would be acting disloyally and deluding one's sovereign. In your servant's foolish opinion, the best thing would be to put him to death.' Paying heed, Huhai had Meng Yi put in bonds at Dai. (Previously he had taken Meng Tian prisoner at Yangzhou.) When the announcement of mourning reached Xianyang and the funeral had taken place, the Crown Prince was set up as Second Generation Emperor and Zhao Gao, being admitted to terms of close intimacy, slandered the Meng family day and night, seeking out their crimes and mistakes so as to recommend their impeachment.

Ziying came forward to remonstrate, saying: 'I hear that in ancient times King Qian of Zhao killed his good minister Li Mu and employed Yan Ju, and King Xi of Yan secretly employed the stratagems of Jing Ke and ignored the pact with Qin, and King Jian of Qi killed loyal ministers from ancient families which had given long-standing service and made use of the counsels of Hou Sheng. Each of these three rulers lost their states* through changing ancient ways so that disaster befell them. Now the Meng family are important officials and counsellors of Qin and yet our sovereign intends to get rid of them all in a single morning, but your servant humbly considers this to be improper. Your servant hears that it is impossible for one who plans frivolously to govern a state and it is impossible for one who exercises wisdom on his own to preserve his ruler. If you put to death loyal servants and set up people who have nothing to do with integrity, then within the palace this will cause all your servants to lose confidence in each other, and in the field it will cause the purposes of your fighting men to lose their cohesion. Your servant humbly considers this to be improper.'

Huhai did not take any notice, but dispatched the imperial scribe Qu Gong to ride relay and go to Dai and instruct Meng Yi as follows: 'You, minister, made things difficult when our previous sovereign wanted to set up a crown prince. Now the Chief Minister considers that you are disloyal, and that your whole clan is implicated in the crime. But in the kindness of Our heart We bestow death* upon you, minister, which is surely extremely gracious. It is for you to give this your consideration!'

'If it is thought that your servant was incapable of grasping the wishes of our previous sovereign,' replied Meng Yi, 'then when he was young he was in his service and obediently received his patronage until he passed away, so it may be said that he knew what he wanted. Or if it is thought that your servant was unaware of the abilities of the Crown Prince, then he went all over the Empire with the Crown Prince in sole attendance, and left all the other princes extremely far behind, so your servant had no doubts. Our previous sovereign's proposal to employ him as crown prince had been building up over several years, so what words would your servant have dared to utter in remonstrance, and what plan would he dare to have devised! It is not that I dare to produce showy verbiage for the purpose of avoiding death and implicate the reputation of our previous sovereign by creating an embarrassment, but I would like you, sir, to devote your thoughts to this, and make sure that the circumstances which cause your servant to be put to death are true. Moreover perfect obedience is what the Way honours, and killing as a punishment is what the Way puts an end to. In former times Duke Mu of Qin died having killed three good men, and charged Baili Xi with a crime although it was not his. Therefore he was given the title of "False".* King Zhaoxiang killed Bai Qi, Lord Wuan. King Ping of Chu killed Wu She. Fucha King of Wu killed Wu Zixu. These four rulers all made major mistakes and so all under Heaven regarded them as wrong and thought such rulers were unenlightened, and as such they were recorded by the feudal lords. Therefore it is said that "Those who govern in accordance with the Way do not kill the guiltless and punishment is not inflicted on the innocent." It is up to you, my lord, to take notice!' But the messengers were aware of what Huhai wanted, so they took no notice of Meng Yi's words, and killed him forthwith.

Second Generation also dispatched messengers to go to Yangzhou, with the following instructions for Meng Tian: 'Your errors, my lord, have become numerous, and your younger brother Yi bears a great burden of guilt, so the law has caught up with you.' 'From my grandfather right down to his sons and grandsons,' said Meng Tian, 'their achievements and trustworthiness have been built up in Qin over three generations. Now your servant has been in command of more than 300,000 soldiers, and although he personally is a prisoner, his influence is sufficient to instigate a revolt. But as one who safeguards righteousness although he is aware he is bound to die, he does not dare to disgrace the teachings of his forebears, and in this way he does not forget his former sovereign. In former times when King Cheng of Zhou was first set on the throne and had not yet left his swaddling clothes, Dan Duke of Zhou carried the King on his back to go to court, and ultimately restored order in all under Heaven. When King Cheng had an illness and was in extreme danger, Duke Dan personally cut his finger-nails and sank the parings in the Yellow River. "The King does not yet possess understanding, and it is I who handle affairs," he said. "If there is a crime-engendered disaster, I accept the unfortunate consequences of it." Accordingly he made an account and stored it away in the repository of records, and he may be said to have behaved with good faith. When the time came when the King was able to govern the country, there was a malicious official who said: "Dan Duke of Zhou has long intended to make a rebellion, and if the King is not prepared, there is bound to be a major crisis." The King was consequently furious and Dan Duke of Zhou ran away and fled to Chu. When King Cheng looked in the repository of records, he got hold of the account of the sinking, and so he said, with tears streaming down his face: "Who said that Dan Duke of Zhou intended to make a rebellion?" He killed the one who had said this and restored Dan Duke of Zhou. Thus the *Book of Zhou* says: "One must put them in threes and fives."* Now for generations my family has avoided duplicity, so if our affairs are finally in such straits, this is bound to be due to the methods of a wicked minister rebelliously stirring up trouble. That King Cheng made a mistake, but when he restored the situation, he ultimately flourished; but Jie killed Guan Longfeng and Zhou killed Prince Bi Gan, and they did not repent, and when they died their country was destroyed. Your servant therefore says that errors can be remedied and remonstrance can be understood. To examine into threes and fives is the method of supreme sages. All in all, your servant's words have not been for the purpose of seeking to escape from blame. He is about to die because he is making a remonstrance, and he wishes Your Majesty would think about following the Way for the sake of the myriad people.' 'Your servants have received an imperial decree to carry out the law on you, general,' said the messengers, 'and they do not dare to report your words to the Supreme One.' Meng Tian sighed deeply. 'For what am I being blamed by Heaven,' he cried, 'that I should die although I have avoided error?' After a good long while he solemnly said: 'There is a crime for which I certainly ought to die. I built a wall stretching more than 10,000 *li* from Lintao as far as Liaodong, and so in the course of this I surely could not avoid cutting through the earth's arteries. This then is my crime.' And so he swallowed poison and killed himself.

The Grand Historiographer says: 'I have been to the northern border and returned via the direct road. On my journey I observed the ramparts of the Great Wall which Meng Tian built for Qin. He hollowed out the mountains and filled in the valleys and opened up a direct road. To be sure, he showed little concern for the efforts of the people. Qin had only just destroyed the feudal states and the hearts of the people of all under Heaven had not yet been restored to order, and the wounded had not yet been healed; but Tian, although he had become a famous general, did not use this occasion to remonstrate strongly and remedy the distresses of the people, minister to the old and enable the orphans to survive, and strive to cultivate harmony among the masses. Instead he embarked on great enterprises to pander to imperial ambition, so was it not therefore reasonable that both he and his brother should suffer the death penalty? Why in that case should cutting the arteries of the earth be made a crime?'

5

THE ANNALS OF QIN

Having translated four biographies which relate to the Qin Dynasty and its ruler, I now turn to the annalistic section of the Historical Records. *Chapters 5 and 6 are devoted to Qin annals, the former dealing almost entirely with the history of the state before the time of King Zheng, who later became First Emperor of the Qin Dynasty. Chapter 6 starts by briefly recounting the early life of Zheng before he unified China. Here we take up the story immediately after the unification.*

Now Qin for the first time had unified all under Heaven and instructions were given to the Chief Minister and the Imperial Secretary saying: 'On another occasion the King of Hann* offered us his territory and handed over his seal, requesting to become a frontier vassal, but having done so he turned his back on the agreement and formed a north–south alliance with Zhao and Wei to rebel against Qin, so we raised troops to punish them and took their king prisoner. I consider this to be a good thing since it practically brought an end to the fighting. The King of Zhao sent his chief minister, Li Mu, to come and arrange a treaty with us, and therefore we returned his hostage-son. But, having done so, he turned his back on the treaty, rebelled against us at Taiyuan, and therefore we raised troops to punish them, and took their king. And then, when Jia Prince of Zhao set himself up as King of Dai, we therefore raised troops to smite and destroy him. The King of Wei first of all guaranteed to surrender and come over to Qin, but having done so he plotted with Hann and Zhao to make a surprise attack on Qin, and officers and soldiers of Qin went to inflict punishment and subsequently defeated him. The King of Chu presented us with the land to the west of Qingyang, but having done so he rebelled against the agreement and attacked us in the Nan province, and so we sent out troops to inflict punishment and took their king, and then restored order to his territory. The King of Yan was stupid and iniquitous, and his crown prince Dan even gave secret orders to Jing Ke to perform a dastardly deed, but the officers and soldiers inflicted punishment and wiped out his state. The King of Qi, taking the advice of Hou Sheng, broke off diplomatic relations with Qin, intending to create chaos, but our officers and soldiers inflicted punishment and took their king prisoner, and restored peace to the territory of Qi. With my own insignificant person I have raised troops to punish violence and chaos and, with the support of the sacred power of the ancestral temples, the six kings have all admitted their crimes, and order is magnificently restored in all under Heaven. Now if the title is not changed there will be no means of praising these achievements and transmitting them to later generations. You are to discuss the imperial title.'

Chief Minister Wang Wan, Imperial Secretary Feng Jie, Superintendent of Trials Li Si, and others all said: 'In days of old the territory of the Five Emperors was 1,000 *li* square, and beyond this was the territory of the feudal princes and of the barbarians. Some of the feudal princes came to court and some did not, for the Son of Heaven was unable to exercise control. Now Your Majesty has raised a righteous army to punish the oppressors and bring peace and order to all under Heaven, so that everywhere within the seas has become our provinces and districts and the laws and ordinances have as a result become unified. This is something which has never once existed from remote antiquity onwards, and which the five Emperors did not attain. Your servants have carefully discussed this with the scholars of broad learning and, as in antiquity there was the Heavenly August, the Earthly August, and the Supreme August, and the Supreme August was the most highly honoured, so your servants, risking death, submit a venerable title, and propose that the King should become "the Supreme August". His commands should be "edicts", his orders should be "decrees", and the Son of Heaven should refer to himself as "the mysterious one".' The King said: 'Omit the word "supreme" and write "august" and pick out the title of "emperor" used from remote antiquity, so that the title will be "August Emperor". The rest shall be as you suggest.' And an edict was issued saying that it should be done. King Zhuangxiang was to be posthumously honoured as 'the Supreme August on High'.

The following edict was issued: 'We have heard that in high antiquity there were titles but no posthumous names. In middle antiquity there were titles, but when people died they were provided with posthumous names in accordance with their conduct. If this is so, then it is a case of the son passing judgement on the father and the subject passing judgement on the ruler. This is quite pointless, and We will not adopt this practice in such matters. Henceforward the law on posthumous names is abolished. We are the first August Emperor and later generations will be numbered in accordance with this system, Second Generation, Third Generation, right down to Ten Thousandth Generation,* and this tradition will continue without end.'

To continue the succession of the Five Powers* the First Emperor considered that, as Zhou had got the Power of Fire and Qin was replacing the Zhou power, it should adopt what fire does not overcome, so it was precisely at this moment that the Power of Water started. The beginning of the year was changed, and the court celebrations all started at the beginning of the tenth month. In all garments, flags, and pennants black was made predominant. And as far as number was concerned they took six as the basis of calculation, so that tallies and law caps were 6 inches, carriages were 6 feet wide, 6 feet equalled a 'pace', and imperial carriages had six horses. The Yellow River was renamed 'the Powerful Water' to inaugurate the Power of Water. Repression was intensive and matters were all decided by the law, for only through harsh treatment and the abandonment of humaneness, kindness, harmony, and righteousness could he accord with the destiny of the five Powers. And so the law was made rigorous, and for a long time no amnesty was declared.

The Chief Minister Wang Wan and others said: 'The states are newly defeated and the territories of Yan, Qi, and Chu are distant, so if we do not establish kings for them there will be no means of bringing order to them. We beg to set up your sons in authority, but it is up to the Supreme One alone to favour us with his agreement.' The First Emperor handed down their suggestion to the ministers, and they all thought this would be expedient. But the Superintendent of Trials Li Si advised: 'Only after an extremely large number of sons and younger brothers and people of the same surname had been enfeoffed by King Wen and King Wu did they win the adherence of the distant, and then they attacked and smote each other and behaved like enemies. And when the feudal states wrought vengeance on each other more and more, the Zhou Son of Heaven was incapable of preventing them. Now all within the seas has been unified thanks to Your Majesty's divine power, and everywhere has been turned into provinces and districts. And if your sons and the successful officials are richly rewarded from the public revenues, that will be quite sufficient to secure easy control. If there is no dissension throughout the Empire, then this is the technique for securing tranquillity. To establish feudal states would not be expedient.' The First Emperor said: 'It is because of the existence of marquises and kings that all under Heaven has shared in suffering from unceasing hostilities. When, thanks to the ancestral temples, all under Heaven has for the first time been brought to order, if states are reintroduced, this will mean the establishment of armies, and it would surely be difficult to seek peace in those places. The advice of the Superintendent of Trials is right.'

So the Empire was divided into thirty-six provinces, and a governor and army commander and an inspector were established for each. The people were renamed 'the black-headed people', and there were great celebrations. The weapons from all under Heaven were gathered in and collected together at Xianyang and were melted down to make bells and stands and twelve statues of men made of metal, each 1,000 piculs in weight,* to be set up in the courts and palaces. All weights and measures were placed under a unified system, and the axle length of carriages was standardized. For writings they standardized the characters.*

The land to the east stretched as far as the sea and Chaoxian, to the west as far as Lintao and Qiangzhong, to the south as far as the land where the doors face north, and in the north they constructed defences along the Yellow River to form the frontier, and along the Yin Mountains as far as Liaodong. One hundred and twenty thousand powerful and wealthy households from all under Heaven were transferred to Xianyang. All the temples together with Zhangtai and Shanglin were to the south of the Wei. Every time Qin destroyed a feudal state, a replica of its palaces and mansions was produced and it was created on the slope north of Xianyang, overlooking the Wei to the south, while eastwards from Yongmen as far as the Jing and Wei there was a series of mansions, connecting walkways, and pavilions. The beautiful women, bells, and drums* which they had obtained from the various states were installed there to fill them.

In the twenty-seventh year the First Emperor toured Longxi and Beidi, went out via Jitou Mountain and passed Huizhong. Then he built the Xin palace south of the Wei, and subsequently it was renamed the Temple of the Apex, to represent the Apex of Heaven. From the Temple of the Apex a roadway went through to Mount Li, and the front hall of the Ganquan palace was built, and they built a walled roadway from Xianyang to connect with it. This year one degree of promotion was bestowed and express roads were constructed.

In the twenty-eighth year the First Emperor travelled eastwards through his provinces and districts and ascended Mount Zouyi. He set up a stone tablet, and after discussion with the various Confucian scholars of Lu an inscription was carved on the stone extolling the virtue of Qin. They also discussed the matter of the *feng* and *shan* sacrifices* and the sacrifices to mountains and rivers. So next he ascended Mount Tai, set up a stone tablet, and made the *feng* sacrifice. As he descended and there was a violent onset of wind and rain, he rested under a tree, which was consequently enfeoffed as fifth-rank grandee.* He made the *shan* sacrifice at Liangfu. The stone tablet* that he had set up was inscribed with the following words:

When the August Emperor came to the throne, he created regulations and made the laws intelligent, and his subjects cherished his instructions.

In the twenty-sixth year of his rule, he for the first time unified all under Heaven, and there were none who did not submit.

In person he made tours of the black-headed people in distant places, climbed this Mount Tai, and gazed all around at the eastern limits.

His servants who were in attendance concentrated on following his footsteps, looked upon his deeds as the foundation and source of their own conduct, and reverently celebrated his achievements and virtue.

As the Way of good government circulates, all creation obtains its proper place, and everything has its laws and patterns.

His great righteousness shines forth with its blessings, to be handed down to later generations, and they are to receive it with compliance and not make changes in it.

The August Emperor is personally sage, and has brought peace to all under Heaven, and has been tireless in government.

Rising early and retiring late, he has instituted long-lasting benefits, and has brought especial glory to instructions and precepts.

His maxims and rules spread all around, and far and near everything has been properly organized, and everyone receives the benefits of his sagely ambitions.

Noble and base have been divided off and made clear, and men and women conform in accordance with propriety, and carefully fulfil their duties.

Private and public are made manifest and distinguished, and nothing is not pure and clean, for the benefit of our heirs and successors.

His influence will last to all eternity, and the decrees he bequeaths will be revered, and his grave admonitions will be inherited for ever.

He then proceeded to the east of Bohai, passed through Huang and Chui, did a complete tour of Mount Cheng, ascended Zhifu, and set up a stone tablet there extolling the virtue of Qin and then left.

He then went south and ascended Langye and, since he greatly enjoyed it, he stayed for three months. Then he moved 30,000 households of the black-headed people to the foot of Langye terrace, giving them tax and labour exemption for twelve years. When he built Langye terrace, he set up a stone inscription extolling the virtue of Qin,* to make clear that he had achieved his ambition. It said:

In his twenty-eighth year, the August Emperor makes a beginning.

Laws and standards are corrected and adjusted, as a means of recording the myriad things.

Thus he clarifies human affairs, and brings concord to father and son.

With sagacity, wisdom, humaneness, and righteousness, he has made manifest all principles.

In the east he has pacified the eastern lands, and thus he has inspected officers and men.

When this task had been magnificently accomplished, he then turned towards the sea.

Through the achievements of the August Emperor, the basic tasks are diligently worked on.

Farming is put first and non-essentials are abolished, and it is the black-headed people who are made wealthy.

All people under Heaven, have heart and mind in unison.

Implements are given a uniform measure, and the characters used in writing are standardized.

Wherever the sun and moon shine, wherever boats and carts carry goods.

Everyone completes his destiny, and nobody does not get what he wants.

He makes things move in accord with the seasons, such is the August Emperor.

To rectify diverse customs, he has traversed land and water.

Feeling sorrow for the black-headed people, he relaxes not morning or evening.

Removing doubt he fixes the laws, so that all understand what they are forbidden to do.

The regional carls have their separate duties, and all government is regulated and made easy.

What is put into practice is bound to be right, and everything goes according to plan.

The intelligence of the August Emperor, oversees and inspects all four quarters.

High and low, noble and base, do not step out of their rank.

Evil and depravity are not allowed, and all strive to be upright and good.

Putting all their effort into both the trivial and the important, nobody dares to be indolent and careless.

Both far and near and both in developed and in obscure places, they concentrate their efforts on being majestic and sturdy.

Upright, correct, sincere, and loyal, they show constancy in their work.

The virtue of our August Emperor, preserves and settles the four extremes.

Punishes disorder and banishes harm, promotes advantage and attracts prosperity.

The practice of economy accords with the seasons, and all creation abounds.

The black-headed people are at peace, and do not employ armour and weapons.

Relations care for each other, and there are absolutely no bandits or robbers.

Joyful recipients of the teachings, they completely understand the framework of the law.

The area within the six directions,* is the August Emperor's land.

To the west it crosses the shifting sands, and in the south takes in the whole of the north-facing households.

In the east there is the eastern sea, and to the north it extends beyond Daxia.

Wherever human footsteps reach, there are none who are not his subjects.

His achievements surpass those of the Five Emperors, and his beneficence even extends to cattle and horses.

No one does not receive the benefit of his virtue, and everyone is at peace in his dwelling-place.

When the King of Qin united and took possession of all under Heaven he took the name of August Emperor. Then he pacified the eastern lands and reached Langye. The noblemen Wang Li Marquis of Wucheng, Wang Ben Marquis of Tongwu; the nobles without fief Zhao Hai Marquis of Jiancheng, Cheng Marquis of Changwu, Feng Wuze Marquis of Wuxin; Chief Minister Wei Lin and Chief Minister Wang Wan; the ministers Li Si and Wang Wu; and the fifth-rank grandees Zhao Ying and Yang Jiu were in attendance. They debated together beside the sea and said: 'The territory of the ancient emperors did not exceed 1,000 *li,* and the feudal lords each guarded his own boundaries. Some attended court and others did not. They committed aggression against each other and were violent and disorderly, and their destructive attacks did not cease. Nevertheless they inscribed bronze and stone in order to provide themselves with a record. The Five Emperors and Three Kings of old were dissimilar from each other in their knowledge and teachings, and their laws and regulations were not clarified. They laid claim to the awe-inspiring support of gods and spirits in order to spread deception in distant places, but the reality did not correspond with the name, and so they did not long endure. Even before they had reached the end of their lives the feudal lords rebelled, and their laws and ordinances did not run.

Now our August Emperor has unified everywhere within the seas, and has turned it into his provinces and districts, and all under Heaven is at peace. He has brought glory to the ancestral temple, embodies the Way and practises virtue, and his venerable title is magnificently fulfilled. We his subjects have joined together to sing the praises of our August Emperor's achievements and virtue and have produced inscriptions on bronze and stone to make them into examples and models.'

Afterwards Xu Shi of Qi and others submitted a memorial saying that in the sea there were three spirit mountains named Penglai, Fangzhang, and Yingzhou, and immortals dwelt on them. They begged to be able to fast and purify themselves and to go off in search of them, together with some youths and maidens. Thereupon Xu Shi was commissioned to send several thousand young boys and girls out to sea to seek immortals.

On the First Emperor's return journey, when he passed Pengcheng he purified himself and prayed and offered sacrifices, wishing to recover the Zhou cauldrons* from the River Si. He made 1,000 men dive into the water in search of them, but they did not find them. So he went south-west and crossed the River Huai and proceeded to Mount Heng and the Nan province. Sailing down the Yangtze, he reached the shrine at Mount Xiang. They encountered a great wind, and were almost unable to cross over. The Supreme One asked his scholars of broad learning: 'What sort of deity is the Lady of the Xiang?' The scholars of broad learning replied: 'We hear that she was the daughter of Yao and the wife of Shun and is buried here.' At that the First Emperor was furious and he made 3,000 convicts cut down all the trees on Mount Xiang, making the mountain naked. The Supreme One then returned from Nan province via the Pass of Wu.

In the twenty-ninth year the First Emperor made a tour in the east. When he reached Bolangsha in Yangwu, he was startled by bandits.* They looked for them but did not find them, so he ordered a grand search throughout the Empire for ten days. He ascended Zhifu and had an inscription made on stone with the following words:

In the twenty-ninth year, the time being in the middle of spring, when the sunny season had just started,

The August Emperor made a tour in the east, and during his travels he ascended Zhifu, and his gaze shone upon the sea.

The servants who were in attendance observed him in admiration, recalled his blessings and glory, and reflected upon and sang the praises of what he initiated.

In creating the government, the great sage established the laws and regulations, and made manifest the guiding principles.

Abroad he taught the feudal lords, gloriously bestowing the blessings of culture, and spreading enlightenment by means of the principles of righteousness.

The Six States remained aloof, insatiable in greed and violence, and the atrocities and killings did not cease.

The August Emperor felt pity for the multitude, and then sent forth chastising armies, and displayed with determination his military power.

He made his punishments just and his conduct sincere, and his awesome glory spread around, and no one did not submit.

He wiped out the strong and violent, rescued the black-headed people, and restored order to the four quarters.

Everywhere he bestowed enlightened laws, and made warp and woof for all under Heaven, to provide a model for all eternity.

He has become great indeed, and within the whole universe we accept and obey his sage-like intent.

All his servants sing the praises of his achievements, and request to inscribe them on stone, so that they may be displayed and handed down as a constant rule.

On the eastern side of it were the words:

In the twenty-ninth year, the August Emperor went on his travels in the spring, and inspected distant regions.

He went as far as the edge of the sea, and then ascended Zhifu, facing the bright morning sun.

As he gazed at that beauty spread out before him, the attendant servants all reflected, and the principles with which he initiated everything became extremely luminous.

When the sage's laws were first promoted, he established purity and principles within the borders, and beyond them punished the violent and strong.

His military might reached everywhere, and shook the four corners, and he captured and destroyed the six kings.

He manifestly unified all under Heaven, and disasters were brought to an end, and he laid aside weapons for all eternity.

The August Emperor with his bright virtue, establishes principles for the whole universe, and is tireless in seeing and listening.

He has established great righteousness, and manifestly provided all the implements, and all have their badges and standards.

Your servants in their offices obey their lot, and each one understands what he is doing, so in their activities there is no suspicion or doubt.

The black-headed people are transformed, far and near share the same standards, and he does far more than imitate antiquity.

Constant duties have been arranged, and heirs and successors will follow the tradition, and long be beneficiaries of the sagely government.

All his servants admire his virtue, respectfully sing the praises of his sage-like ardour, and beg to set up this inscription at Zhifu.

On his return journey he then went to Langye and returned to the capital via Shangdang.

In the thirtieth year there was no incident.

In the thirty-first year in the twelfth month the winter sacrifice was renamed 'the Felicitous and Equable'.* There was bestowed on the black-headed people 6 piculs of grain and two sheep per village. The First Emperor made a journey incognito in Xianyang, accompanied by four armed guards. Going out at night, they encountered robbers at Lanchi and he was in a sorry predicament, but the guards attacked and killed the robbers, and for twenty days a great search was made in the area within the passes. Rice was 1,600 a picul.

In the thirty-second year the First Emperor went to Jieshi and made Master Lu of Yan search for Xianmen and Gaoshi. An inscription was written on the gate of Jieshi. (Its walls had been pulled down and its fortifications opened up.) The inscription said:

Then he mobilized armies, and punished the unprincipled, and those who perpetrated rebellion were wiped out.

Armed force exterminates the violent and rebellious, but civil power relieves the guiltless of their labours, and the masses all submit in their hearts.

Achievements and toil are generously assessed, and the rewards even extend to cattle and horses, and his bounty enriches the land.

The August Emperor gave a vigorous display of his authority, and his virtue brought together all the states, and for the first time brought unity and supreme peace.

City walls were demolished, waterways were opened up, and obstacles were flattened.

When the physical features of the land had been determined, there was no conscript labour for the masses, and all under Heaven was pacified.

Men take pleasure in their farm-land, and women cultivate their tasks, and all matters have their proper arrangement.

His kindness protects all production, and for long they have been coming together in the fields, and everyone is content with his place.

All his servants sing the praises pf his glory, and beg to inscribe this stone, so as to pass on his example.

Next he sent Han Zhong, Hou Gong, and Master Shi to search for the immortals and the elixir of everlasting life. The First Emperor toured the northern frontier, returning via the Shang province. Master Lu, a man from Yan, returned from his mission to sea, and taking it to be the work of ghosts and spirits submitted a prophetic document which said: 'The one which will destroy Qin will be Hu.'* The First Emperor accordingly ordered General Meng Tian to send out 300,000 troops to go north and attack the Hu, and they captured the territory to the south of the Yellow River.

In the thirty-third year men who had once absconded, or who were useless sons-in-law, or were traders* were sent forth to capture the territory of Luliang. Guilin, Xiang province, and Nanhai were created and convicts were sent to garrison them. In the north-west the Xiongnu were driven back. The area from Yuzhong eastwards along the Yellow River was attached to the Yin Mountains, making forty-four districts, and walls were built along the river as frontier defences. Then Meng Tian was sent across the Yellow River to take Gaoque, Mount Tao, and Beijia. Outposts were built in order to repel the Rong people. And convicts were transported to populate the newly established districts. As a result of a prohibition they could not offer sacrifices. The Morning Star appeared in the west. In the thirty-fourth year judicial officials who had behaved improperly were banished either to build the Great Wall or go to the territory of Southern Yue.

The First Emperor arranged a banquet in the palace at Xianyang, and the seventy scholars of broad learning came into his presence to wish him long life. The Chief Administrator of these scholars, Zhou Qingchen, came forward to offer eulogies, saying: 'At another time Qin territory did not exceed 1,000 *li*, but now thanks to Your Majesty's divine power and brilliant sagacity the area within the seas has been restored to order and the barbarian tribes driven off. Wherever the sun and moon shine no one does not offer his submission. The feudal states have been made into provinces and districts, individuals are contented and pleased with themselves, and there is no worry about war and conflict, and this will be handed down for 10,000 generations. Since high antiquity Your Majesty's authority and virtue have not been matched.'

The First Emperor was pleased. Then the scholar of broad learning Chunyu Yue, a man of Qi, stepped forward and said: 'Your servant has heard that the fact that the Yin and Zhou reigned for more than 1,000 years was because they enfeoffed their sons and younger brothers and successful officials to provide branches and supports for themselves. Now although Your Majesty possesses all within the seas, your sons and younger brothers are private individuals; and ultimately if you have such subordinates as Tian Chang* or the six ministers, if there is no one to offer support and assistance, how will you rescue each other? That an enterprise can survive for long if it is not modelled on antiquity is not anything I have heard about. Now Qingchen is also flattering you to your face so as to aggravate Your Majesty's mistakes. This is not behaving like a loyal subject.'

When the First Emperor passed down his comments Chief Minister Li Si said: 'The Five Emperors did not repeat each other and the Three Dynasties did not copy each other, yet each enjoyed good government. It is not that they were going against each other, but because times change. Now Your Majesty has created a great enterprise and constructed an achievement which will last for 10,000 generations, which is certainly not something which a foolish Confucian would understand. Moreover what Yue is referring to is just the activities of the Three Dynasties, but they are surely not worth being taken as precedents. In other times the feudal lords were in competition with each other to give a generous welcome to itinerant men of learning. But now all under Heaven has been restored to order and the laws and ordinances derive from a single source. The common people at home put their effort into farming and handicrafts, and the public servants on the other hand study the laws and prohibitions. Now all the scholars do not take the present as a model but study antiquity, and thus they reject the present generation and throw the black-headed people into confusion. As chief minister your servant Li Si speaks out at risk of death: in antiquity all under Heaven was divided and in chaos, and nobody could unify it, and it was for this reason that the feudal lords became active together, and in their utterances all spoke of the past to injure the present, and they made a display of empty verbiage in order to throw the truth into confusion. People approved what they had learnt in private in order to reject what their superiors had laid down. Now the August Emperor has unified and taken possession of all under Heaven. You have distinguished white from black and established a single focus of adulation. But those who have studied privately collaborate with each other to reject the laws and teachings, and when people hear ordinances promulgated everyone criticizes them in accordance with his own studies. Indoors they mentally reject them and outside they make criticisms in the byways. They brag to their sovereign in order to make a reputation. Disagreement they regard as noble, and they encourage all the lower orders to fabricate slander. If such things are not prohibited, then above the sovereign's power will decline, and below factions will form. To prohibit this would be expedient.

'Your servant requests that the records of the historians apart from those of Qin should all be burnt.* Apart from those copies which the scholars of broad learning are responsible for in their official capacity, anyone in all under Heaven who dares to possess and hide away the *Songs*, the *Documents*, and the sayings of the hundred schools, should hand them all over to a governor or commandant and they should be indiscriminately burnt. If there is anyone who dares to mention the *Songs* or *Documents* in private conversation, he should be executed. Those who, using the old, reject the new will be wiped out together with their clans. Officers who see and become aware of such cases but do not report them should be convicted of the same crime with them. If thirty days after the ordinance has been promulgated the books are not burnt, then the culprit should be branded and sent to do forced labour on the walls. There should be exemption for books concerned with medicine, pharmacy, divination by tortoiseshell and milfoil, the sowing of crops, and the planting of trees. If anyone intends to make a study of the laws and ordinances, he should take the law officers as teachers.' This proposal was sanctioned by decree.

In the thirty-fifth year a road was opened via Jiuyuan as far as Yunyang. Hills were hollowed out and valleys filled in to make it run straight. Thereupon the First Emperor considered that Xianyang had too many people and that the palaces and courts of the former kings were small. 'I have heard', he said, 'that King Wen of Zhou made his capital at Feng and King Wu made his capital at Hao, so the region between Feng and Hao is a fit seat for an emperor or king. So he constructed a palace for the court in the Shanglin park south of the Wei. First of all he built the front hall, Epang, which was 500 paces* from east to west and 500 feet from north to south. In the upper part it could seat a myriad people, and in the lower part one could erect a 50 foot banner. For transport round about there was a screened highway from below the hall straight to the Southern Mountains. The summit of the Southern Mountains was put on show and treated as the entrance gate. They made a covered way going across the Wei from Epang to reach Xianyang in imitation of the screened highway from the Apex of Heaven which crosses the Milky Way and reaches the Encampment.* The Epang palace was not yet finished; but when it was finished he wanted to make a fresh choice and name it with a good name. But because the palace was built at Epang, the whole world called it the Epang palace. More than 700,000 men who had been castrated or were convict-labourers were in fact divided between building the Epang palace and constructing Mount Li. Stone for the tomb got out of the northern mountains, and timber transported from Shu and Chu both came. Within the passes 300 palaces were planned, and outside the passes more than 400. So they set up a stone beside the Eastern Sea within the boundaries of Qu, to make it the eastern gateway of Qin. Accordingly 30,000 families were shifted to the city of Li and 50,000 to Yunyang, with ten years' exemption from taxation and service in both cases.

Master Lu said to the First Emperor: 'Your servant and others search for the magic fungus, rare elixirs, and immortals, but we constantly fail to come across them. There seems to be something which is harming us. One of the arts of magic is that the sovereign should sometimes travel about in secret in order to avoid evil spirits, for if evil spirits are avoided a true being will come. If subjects know where the sovereign dwells, then this is harmful to his spiritual power. A true being enters water but is not made wet, enters fire but is not burnt, traverses clouds and vapours, and lasts as long as Heaven and Earth. Now the Supreme One governs all under Heaven but cannot yet find tranquillity. I wish that people were not permitted to know the palace where the Supreme One is staying, for only then may the elixir of everlasting life perhaps be found.'

Thereupon the First Emperor said: 'I desire to become a true being, so I shall call myself "true being", and shall not use the term "the mysterious one".' Then he ordered that the 270 palaces and pavilions built within a radius of 200 *li* from Xianyang should be interconnected by causeways and covered walks, and filled with hangings, bells, drums, and beautiful women,* each to stay in its position and not be shifted around. And if anyone mentioned the place which he honoured with his presence as he moved about, he would be condemned to death.

When the First Emperor favoured the Mount Liang palace with a visit, he saw from up on the mountain the large number of the Chief Minister's carriages and outriders, and he did not approve of this. One of the palace eunuchs told the Chief Minister, and afterwards the Chief Minister reduced the number of carriages and outriders, and the First Emperor said angrily: 'This is because an eunuch leaks what I say.' But when they were interrogated, nobody admitted it, so he soon proclaimed that everyone who was in attendance on him at the time should be arrested, and they were all put to death. As a result of this nobody afterwards knew where he was when he travelled about. But whenever he attended to business and his various officials received his decisions, both of these activities took place at the palace at Xianyang.

Master Hou and Master Lu plotted together saying: 'The First Emperor is the sort of person whose heavenly nature is stubborn and self-satisfied. Starting as a feudal lord, he has unified all under Heaven, and now that his ambitions have been fulfilled and his desires obeyed he thinks that since antiquity nobody has matched himself. He only puts his trust in the law officers, and it is they who win his intimacy and favours. Although there are seventy scholars of broad learning, they are there only to make up the number and he does not take their advice. The Chief Minister and the other important officials all accept business which has been already dealt with and they depend on decisions being made by the Supreme One. The Supreme One enjoys using punishments and executions as a sign of his authority, and since all under Heaven hang on to their salaries in fear of punishment, nobody dares to fulfil his loyal duties. Since the Supreme One does not hear about his faults, he grows daily more arrogant, and his subordinates, cringing in terror, practise duplicity in order to win his forbearance. According to Qin law, one cannot practise more than one kind of magic, and if one does not offer proof one is immediately put to death. What is more, those who watch the stars and vapours have reached 300 in number, and all are good scholars, but in their terror they conceal the truth and utter compliments, and do not dare to speak out about his faults. The business of the Empire, no matter whether trivial or important, is all decided by the Supreme One, who goes so far as to have the documents weighed, so that he cannot rest until he has dealt with the right number of documents for that day and night. When his greed for authority has reached such a pitch, the elixir of immortality can never be sought for him.' Thereupon they fled.

When the Emperor heard of their disappearance, he flew into a great rage and said: 'Previously I collected together the writings of all under Heaven and got rid of all which were useless. I called together all the scholars and magicians, an extremely large gathering, intending to promote an era of great peace by this means, and the magicians I intended to pick out to go in search of strange elixirs. Now I hear that Han Zhong has left and not made a report, and the expenses of Xu Shi and his colleagues may be reckoned in millions, but they have totally failed to obtain elixirs, and it is only the charges of corruption they make against each other which I hear of daily. I was extremely generous in the honours and gifts I bestowed on Master Lu and the others, but now they even slander me so as to emphasize the fact that I am not virtuous. I have had

people investigate all the scholars who are in Xianyang, and some
have been fabricating weird rumours in order to confuse the black-
headed people.'

Thereupon he made the Imperial Secretary investigate all the
scholars, who were reported to have informed on each other; but
in fact, although they tried to exonerate themselves, more than
460 who had infringed the prohibitions were all buried alive at
Xianyang, and the whole Empire was made to know about this to
serve as a warning for the future. And increasingly people were
banished to the frontiers. Fusu, the eldest son of the First Emperor,
remonstrated and said: 'All under Heaven has only just been restored
to order and the black-headed people in the distant regions have
not yet been brought together, and all the scholars sing the praises
of Master Kong* and adopt him as a model, but now the Supreme
One restrains them all by emphasizing the law, and your servant
is afraid that all under Heaven will not be at peace. It is up to the
Supreme One to investigate this.' The First Emperor was angry,
and he made Fusu go north and act as inspector of Meng Tian in
the Shang province.

In the thirty-sixth year Mars was stationed in the mansion of the
Heart.* There was a meteor which fell in the Dong province, and
when it reached the earth it turned into a stone, and someone among
the black-headed people inscribed the stone concerned with the
words: 'When the First Emperor dies, the land will be divided up.'
When the First Emperor heard this, he sent the Imperial Secretary
to investigate and, when nobody confessed, all those who lived near
the stone were taken and condemned to death, and as a consequence
the stone concerned was destroyed by burning.

The First Emperor was not happy, and he made the scholars
of broad learning compose poems about immortals and true beings
and also on wherever in the Empire he went on his travels, and
musicians were instructed to sing and play them. That autumn
an envoy coming from east of the passes was travelling along the
Pingshu road in Huayin at night when he was accosted by a man carrying a jade disc, who said: 'Give this to the Lord of Haochi for me.'
By way of explanation he added: 'This year the ancestral dragon
will die.' When the envoy asked the reason for this, as a result he

suddenly disappeared, putting his jade disc down as he left. The envoy presented the disc and told him the whole story. The First Emperor seemed preoccupied for a good long time. Then he said: 'Mountain spirits assuredly know only the events of a single year.' But after he had withdrawn he said: 'The ancestral dragon means the first among men.' He made the imperial treasury have a look at the jade, and it was in fact the one that he had thrown into the Yangtze River as he went across it on his travels during the twenty-eighth year. Then the First Emperor consulted the tortoiseshell* about it, and the response he got was that it was a propitious time both for touring and for transportation. And 30,000 families were removed to Beihe and Yuzhong. And these people were promoted one degree in rank.

In the tenth month of the thirty-seventh year on the day *guichou** the First Emperor set out on tour. The Chief Minister of the Left, Li Si, was in attendance, but the Chief Minister of the Right, Feng Quji, remained behind to look after things. A younger son, Huhai, of whom he was extremely fond, requested to join the company, and the Supreme One agreed to this. In the eleventh month they reached Yunmeng on their journey and a sacrifice was made to Emperor Shun on Mount Jiuyi. They sailed down the Yangtze, inspected Jike and crossed Haizhu, passed Danyang and reached Qiantang. When he approached the River Zhe, the waves were terrible, so he went in a westerly direction for 20 *li* to cross where the river was narrower. They ascended Kuaiji, and a sacrifice was made to the great Yu. They also sacrificed to the southern sea, and set up a stone tablet with an inscription extolling the virtue of Qin. The text of it was:

The August Emperor, glorious in the blessings he brought, pacified and unified everywhere within the universe, and his virtue and kindness will long survive.

In his thirty-seventh year, he in person toured all under Heaven, and everywhere inspected the distant regions.

Then he ascended Kuaiji, and examined the customs and practices, and the black-headed people showed their reverence.

All his servants sing the praises of his achievements, and as they trace his deeds from the beginning, they reflect upon his lofty radiance.

When the sage of Qin took charge of his state, he first determined punishments and names, and clearly set forth the ancient regulations.

He was the first to standardize the system of laws,* examine and demarcate duties and responsibilities, so as to establish unchanging practices.

But the six kings devoted their attention to rebelliousness; they were greedy, oppressive, insolent, and fierce; and led the multitudes and made themselves strong.

In their violence they behaved wantonly and, trusting to their strength, they were arrogant, and they often brought armour and weapons into action.

They secretly dispatched spies far and wide, and through their activities formed north–south alliances, and in their conduct practised evil methods.

At home they glossed over their underhand plots, and abroad they came and invaded our borders, consequently stirring up disaster.

They were punished justly and with authority, their cruel rebelliousness was obliterated, and the criminals who spread disorder were wiped out.

The sage-like virtue is widespread and intense, and everyone in the six directions, gains the benefit of limitless blessings.

The August Emperor has unified the universe, and he pays attention to all of the myriad concerns, and both near and far are made pure.

He introduces principle to all things, investigates the reality of matters, and everything bears its own name.*

He comprehends both noble and base, and the good and not good are ranged before him, so that they do not have secret natures.

He glosses over mistakes and spreads righteousness, but if a woman remarries when she has a son, then she turns her back on the dead and is not upright.

Taking precautions, he helps separate off the internal and the external and bans licentiousness, so men and women are pure and sincere.

If a man commits adultery, to kill him is no crime, so men hang on to the standards of righteousness.

If a wife elopes to remarry, then the son will not have a mother, and so everyone is converted into chastity and purity.

His great rule cleanses morality, and all under Heaven come under his influence, and are the beneficiaries of his bountiful regime.

Everyone honours the rules, and earnestly strives in harmony and tranquillity, and nobody does not obey orders.

The black-headed people cultivate purity, men delight in sharing the same model, and are happy to guard the great peace.

Posterity will accept the law with respect, and perpetual government will have no ending, and carts and boats will not be overturned.

The servants who are in attendance extol his splendid achievement, and beg to inscribe this stone tablet, conspicuously to transmit a monument to his beneficence.

On his return he passed Wu, crossed the river from Jiangcheng, went along the sea coast and, travelling northwards, reached Langye. The magician Xu Shi and others had gone to sea in search of spirit elixirs, but after several years had not obtained any, and the expenses had been heavy, so they were afraid of being reprimanded. Accordingly they made up a false story, saying: 'The elixirs can be obtained on Penglai, but we are always harassed by huge sharks and so cannot get there. We would like to request that skilful archers go along with us, so that when they see them they will shoot them with repeating crossbows.'

The First Emperor dreamed that he was having a fight with a sea spirit in human form. When he asked the scholars of broad learning about the interpretation of the dream, they said: 'Water spirits cannot be seen, but they make themselves into a huge fish or water-dragon to lie in wait. Now although the Supreme One has been thorough in his prayers and sacrifices, nevertheless this evil spirit exists and it is necessary to banish it so that good spirits may be summoned.' So he ordered those who went to sea to provide implements for catching an enormous fish, and he himself lay in wait with a repeating crossbow to shoot at the huge fish when it appeared. From Langye he went north as far as Mount Rongcheng, but did not see it. But when he reached Zhifu he saw some enormous fish, and he shot and killed one of them. Then he went westwards along the sea coast.

When he reached Pingyuan ford he fell ill. The First Emperor hated to talk about death, so none of his ministers dared to mention the matter of death. When the Supreme One's illness became more serious, he composed a letter under the imperial seal to be bestowed on Prince Fusu saying: 'Take part in my funeral at Xianyang and see to the burial.' When the letter had been sealed, it was kept in the place where Director of Palace Coach-houses Zhao Gao dispatched business under imperial seal, but it had not yet been handed over to a messenger. In the seventh month on *bingyin* the First Emperor passed away at Pingtai in Shaqiu. Because the Supreme One had passed away while outside the capital, Chief Minister Li Si was afraid that there would be rebellion among the various princes and also in the Empire, and so he kept it a secret, and did not announce the mourning. The coffin was borne in a sleeping-carriage, and so the favourite eunuchs attended the carriage, and wherever they came to, food was sent in. The various officials submitted business as before, whereupon the eunuchs immediately approved all the submitted business from within the sleeping-carriage. Only the son Huhai and Zhao Gao, together with five or six favourite eunuchs, knew that the Supreme One was dead. Zhao Gao had formerly taught Huhai writing and matters of law and the administration of justice, and Huhai privately favoured him. Zhao Gao accordingly joined with Prince Huhai and Chief Minister Li Si and secretly plotted to destroy the letter that the First Emperor had sealed for bestowal on Prince Fusu. In its place they fabricated a testamentary edict which Chief Minister Li Si was supposed to have received from the First Emperor at Shaqiu, appointing his son Huhai as crown prince. The letter was rewritten and bestowed on Fusu and Meng Tian, charging them with crimes and bestowing death upon them. (This is described in detail in the biography of Li Si.*) They went on their journey and subsequently went via Jingxing to Jiuyuan. It happened to be hot weather and the Supreme One's sleeping-carriage stank, and so there was an imperial mandate to the effect that the attendant officials should have carts loaded with a picul of salted fish in order to disguise the smell of it.

Continuing on their journey, they took the direct road back to Xianyang and announced the mourning. Crown Prince Huhai succeeded to the throne and became Second Generation Emperor. In the ninth month the First Emperor was buried at Mount Li.* When the First Emperor had just come to the throne, excavations and building work had taken place at Mount Li, but when he unified all under Heaven, convicts to the number of more than 700,000 were sent there from all over the Empire. They dug through three springs and poured down molten bronze to make the outer coffin; and replicas of palaces, pavilions, all the various officials, and wonderful vessels, and other rare objects were brought up to the tomb, which was then filled with them. Craftsmen were ordered to make crossbows and arrows which would operate automatically, so that anyone who approached what had been excavated was immediately shot. Quicksilver was used to represent the various waterways, the Yangtze and Yellow Rivers, and the great sea, being made by some mechanism to flow into each other, and above were ranged the heavenly constellations and below was the layout of the land. Candles were made of whale fat, for it was reckoned that it would be a long time before they were extinguished.

Second Generation said: 'It would not be right that any of the previous Emperor's concubines should emerge from this place unless she has a son.' They were all ordered to accompany him in death, and those who died were extremely numerous. After the burial had taken place someone mentioned the fact that the workers and craftsmen who had constructed the mechanical devices would know about all the buried treasures and the importance of the treasures would immediately be disclosed. Consequently when the great occasion was finished and after the treasures had been hidden away, the main entrance way to the tomb was shut off, and the outer gate lowered, so that all the workers and craftsmen who had buried the treasure were shut in, and there were none who came out again. And vegetation and trees were planted to make it look like a hill.

In Second Generation's first year he was 21 years old. Zhao Gao became Director of Palace Gentlemen, and he was given responsibility for the conduct of affairs. Second Generation sent down a decree that the ritual concerning the sacrificial victims at the mortuary temple of the First Emperor, together with the various sacrifices to the hills and rivers, should be enhanced. He ordered all the officials to discuss the question of venerating the temple of the First Emperor. The ministers all bowed their heads and said: 'In antiquity the Son of Heaven had seven temples, the feudal lords had five, and the grandees had three, and this will not be superseded even after 10,000 generations. Now the First Emperor's temple is considered supreme, and everyone within the four seas offers tribute and the number of sacrificial victims has been increased. The ritual is all perfect and there is nothing to add. But of the temples of the previous kings some are in Yong and some are in Xianyang, and by rights only the Son of Heaven ought to offer libations and sacrifices at the temple to the First Emperor. All those from Duke Xiang onwards are superseded. The establishment consists in all of seven temples, and all the officials should enter these and sacrifice in accordance with the ritual, so that the ancestral temple of the First Emperor is venerated as the ancestral temple of those who have been emperors. And the August Emperor should again call himself "the mysterious one".

Making plans with Zhao Gao, Second Generation said: 'I am young and have only just ascended the throne, so the black-headed people have not yet got together and formed an attachment to me. The previous Emperor toured the provinces and districts so as to display his might and overawe all within the seas into submission. If I now behave in a retiring manner and do not go on tour, then I shall appear weak, and will have no means of reducing all under Heaven to subjection.' In spring Second Generation journeyed east to the provinces and districts and Li Si was in attendance. He went to Jieshi, and then went along the sea coast southwards until they came to Kuaiji, and wrote an inscription on all the inscribed stones set up by the First Emperor, writing on the sides of the tablets the names of the important ministers who were in attendance, so as to manifest on them the previous Emperor's accomplishments and copious virtue:

The August Emperor said: 'These inscriptions on bronze and stone were all made by the First Emperor. Now I have succeeded to his title and, since the wording of the bronze and stone inscriptions does not mention the First Emperor, then in the remote future it may seem as if his successors made these, and his accomplishments and copious virtue will not be praised.' So the Chief Ministers Li Si and Feng Quji and Imperial Secretary De, risking death, said: 'Your servants request that the imperial decree should all be written up on the inscribed stone, and consequently it will become clear. Risking death, your servants make this request.' And an imperial decree said that this should be done.

Subsequently they went on to Liaodong and returned.

Thereupon Second Generation, accepting the advice of Zhao Gao, expanded the laws and ordinances. Having secretly plotted together with Zhao Gao, he said: 'The important officials do not give me their submission and the bureaucracy is still powerful, and the princes are bound to be at odds with me, so what shall I do about it?' 'Your servant definitely wanted to speak,' said Gao, 'but never dared to. The important officials of the previous Emperor all came from famous and noble families, known throughout all under Heaven for countless generations, and for a long time they have accumulated achievements and won glory in their generations so that these things have been handed down from one to another. Now I am obscure and lowly by origin, but Your Majesty has favoured me with promotion and caused me to be in a senior position, in control of affairs within the palace. The important officials are discontented and accept your servant's leadership only in appearance, and in their hearts they truly do not submit. Now when the Supreme One leaves the capital, he does not avail himself of this opportunity to investigate those among the civil and military governors of provinces and districts who have committed crimes and punish them. By this means the Supreme One would both overawe all under Heaven and at the same time get rid of those whom he spends his whole life disparaging. At the present moment things do not model themselves on civil virtues but are decided by military strength. I wish Your Majesty would consequently make the best of the circumstances and do away with hesitation, and then all your officials will not get so far as to make plots. If as an intelligent sovereign you gather together and promote the interests of the rest of the people, ennobling the humble and enriching the poor and bringing close those who are far away, then both high and low will come together and the state will be made tranquil.'

'Good,' said Second Generation. So he proceeded to execute important officials and princes, and the low-ranking officials close to the throne and the three grades of palace gentlemen were arrested for complicity in their crimes and errors, and nobody could stand up to this. Indeed six princes were put to death at Du. Prince Jianglü and two brothers were imprisoned in the inner palace, and the discussion of their crimes came last of all. Second Generation sent a messenger to give instructions to Jianglü, saying: 'The prince does not behave as a subject should behave, and for this crime he merits the death penalty, and the officers will carry out the law on him.' Jianglü said: 'In court ritual I have never once dared not to follow the Assistant of Guests; in taking my place in the hall of state I have never once dared to neglect ceremony; and in receiving orders and responding to them I have never once dared to make a mistake in my words. What is meant by my not behaving as a true subject? I would like to hear what I am found guilty of before I die.' The messenger said: 'Your servant cannot discuss it with you. I have received a letter and am carrying out what has to be done.' Jianglü then looked up to Heaven and cried out to it three times in a loud voice: 'Is it Heaven? For I am not guilty!' The three brothers then all wept, drew their swords, and killed themselves. The royal family was terrified. Anyone among the officials who remonstrated was considered to be uttering slanders, and the important officers hung on to their salaries and tried to put on appearances, and the black-headed people were terrified.

In the fourth month, when Second Generation returned and reached Xianyang, he said: 'Because the court at Xianyang was small, the previous Emperor therefore built the palace of Epang to provide a residence, but before it was completed it so happened that the Supreme One passed away, so the workers were disbanded, but they were re-engaged to replace the earth at Mount Li. The work at Mount Li is largely complete, so if I now abandoned the Epang palace and did not make progress on it, then this would indicate that the previous Emperor was wrong to undertake the task.' So they again worked on the Epang palace. And away from the capital they pacified the barbarians on all sides in accordance with the First Emperor's plan. He summoned 50,000 picked troops altogether to encamp and guard Xianyang, and they were made to teach archery and the hunting of wild animals with dogs and horses. But as there were many who had to be fed and it was calculated that there was not enough food, so orders were sent down that provinces and districts were to transport pulse, grain, and fodder and everyone was told to bring along his own food supplies, and everywhere within

300 *li* of Xianyang people could not consume their own grain. And the enforcement of the law became harsher.

In the seventh month the frontier soldier Chen Sheng and others rebelled in the former territory of Chu and they became the 'magnifiers of Chu'. Sheng set himself up as King of Chu and established his seat at Chen, and sent out various generals to acquire territory. The young men of the provinces and districts east of the mountains had suffered harsh treatment from Qin law officers, so they rebelled, killing all their governors, commandants, magistrates, and their aides, so as to respond to Chen Sheng's actions. They set each other up as marquises and kings and, forming alliances, countless numbers of them headed in a westerly direction, ostensibly for the sake of attacking Qin. When an imperial messenger came from the east to report the rebellion* to Second Generation, he was furious and handed him over to the law officers. Later on, when envoys came and were questioned by the Supreme One, they replied saying: 'The bands of robbers have just been repelled or captured by the governor or commandant of the province, and now that they have all been got hold of, they are not worth worrying about.' The Supreme One was pleased. Wu Chen set himself up as King of Zhao, Wei Jiu as King of Wei, and Tian Dan as King of Qi. The Governor of Pei rose up in Pei, and Xiang Liang raised troops in the province of Kuaiji.

In winter in the second year Zhou Zhang and other generals sent by Chen Sheng had marched westward and reached Xi with several hundred thousand soldiers. Second Generation was seriously alarmed and consulted all his officials about what he should do. The lesser treasurer Zhang Han said: 'The bandits have already arrived and they are numerous and strong, and if we send forth forces now from the nearby districts it will not be good enough. But there are many convicts on Mount Li and I beg that they be granted an amnesty and given weapons so as to smite them.' Second Generation accordingly proclaimed a major amnesty throughout the Empire, appointed Zhang Han as general and he smote and defeated the army of Zhou Zhang and put it to flight, and subsequently Zhou Zhang was killed at Caoyang. Second Generation then also sent the senior scribes Sima Xin and Dong Yi to help Zhang Han smite the bandits, and they killed Chen Sheng at Chengfu, and smashed Xiang Liang at Dingtao, and wiped out Wei Jiu at Linji. When the most famous leaders of the bandits from the territory of Chu had died, Zhang Han consequently went north and crossed the Yellow River and smote Xie King of Zhao and others at Julu.

Zhao Gao said to Second Generation: 'The previous Emperor administered the Empire for a long time, and so all the officials did not dare to do wrong or introduce unorthodox suggestions. Now Your Majesty has a rich store of springs and autumns to come but has only just ascended the throne, so how can you decide matters at court in the presence of the ministers of state? Once you have made a mistake in dealing with business, it will demonstrate your shortcomings to all the officials. The Son of Heaven refers to himself as "the mysterious one" and therefore he does not let his voice be heard.' Thereupon Second Generation stayed constantly within the forbidden precincts and took decisions on all business together with Gao. After this the ministers of state were rarely able to attend court or obtain audience.

The bandits and brigands became ever more numerous, and troops from within the passes were ceaselessly sent eastwards to smite them. Quji, the Chief Minister of the Right, and Li Si, the Chief Minister of the Left, and General Feng Jie came forward and remonstrated. 'In the area east of the passes bands of brigands have risen up together,' they said, 'and when Qin sends out troops to punish and smite them, those whom we kill and put to flight are extremely numerous, but nevertheless they do not stop. The number of bandits is due to the fact that all who are engaged in the activities of manning the frontiers or transporting goods suffer hardship, and taxation is heavy. We request that for the future you halt the construction of the Epang palace, and reduce frontier-guarding duties and transport service on all frontiers.'

Second Generation said: 'I heard the following from Master Han: "Yao and Shun neither polished their oak rafters nor trimmed their thatched hut, and they ate and drank from earthenware bowls, so that even a gatekeeper's nourishment is not more frugal than this. When Yu forced a passage through Longmen and made a way through Daxia to release the stagnant waters of the Yellow River and allowed them to flow into the sea, he carried rammer and spade himself, and his shins were hairless. The labours of a slave are not more arduous than this." But all the things on account of which one is honoured in that one possesses the Empire consist of being able to indulge one's desires and take one's wishes to the extreme, for if the sovereign stresses making the laws clear, subordinates will not dare to do wrong, so that in that way he may administer all within the seas. If sovereigns like Shun and Yu are honoured as Sons of Heaven, but themselves dwell in impoverished and harsh circumstances and publicize this to the common people, then one must still ask what good they are as models.

'We are honoured as the ruler of 10,000 chariots, but do not have the reality of this, so We intend to create a force of 1,000 chariots or even to have an attachment of 10,000 chariots, so that We may fulfil Our title. Moreover the previous Emperor started off as a feudal lord, but unified all under Heaven, and when all under Heaven had been brought to order, he drove off the barbarians on all four sides in order to bring peace to the frontiers, built palaces and mansions in order to demonstrate that he had obtained his ambition, and you, my lords, observed that the previous Emperor's achievements took place in proper sequence. But within two years of Our ascending the throne, bands of brigands have risen up together, and you, my lords, are incapable of preventing this, and you even want me to abandon what the previous Emperor was doing. Thus on the one hand you dispense with the means of repaying the previous Emperor, and on the other hand you are not fully exerting your loyalty and strength on Our behalf. So how is it that you are in office?' He handed over Quji, Si, and Jie to the law officers, and their responsibility for other crimes was investigated. Quji and Jie said: 'Generals and chief ministers do not accept disgrace,' and killed themselves. But ultimately Si remained a prisoner and underwent the five punishments.

In the third year Zhang Han and others led their troops to lay siege to Julu, and Xiang Yu, the Supreme General of Chu, commanding Chu troops, went to the relief of Julu. In winter Zhao Gao became chief minister, and completed the investigation of Li Si and killed him.

In summer Zhang Han and others fought battles but on several occasions were driven back, so Second Generation sent someone to reprimand Han, and he was afraid and sent his senior scribe Xin to ask advice on the matter. But Zhao Gao did not give him an interview, and also did not have confidence in him. Xin fled in terror, but when Gao sent people to pursue and capture him they did not overtake him. When Xin had an interview with Han he said: 'Zhao Gao is in control of whatever happens in the palace, and you will be put to death, general, whether you are successful or not.' So when Xiang Yu suddenly smote the Qin army and took Wang Li prisoner, Han and others then surrendered with their soldiers to the feudal states.

In the eighth month on *jihai* Zhao Gao wanted to bring about a rebellion, but was afraid that the officials would not pay heed, so he first of all arranged a test. He took a deer* and presented it to Second Generation and said: 'It is a horse.' Second Generation smiled and said: 'Have you not got it wrong, Chief Minister? You said a deer was a horse.' He asked the courtiers, and some of them remained silent, while others said it was a horse in order to curry favour with Zhao Gao, and others said it was a deer. So Zhao Gao secretly had the law on all who said it was a deer. Afterwards the officials were all afraid of Gao.

Previously Gao had said on several occasions that there was nothing that the bandits east of the passes were capable of doing. But now we have reached the time when Xiang Yu took prisoner the Qin general Wang Li and others at Julu and proceeded to advance, and the army of Zhang Han and others was driven back on several occasions and had submitted memorials requesting reinforcements, and Yan, Zhao, Qi, Chu, Hann, and Wei had all been set up as kingdoms, while generally speaking the area east of the passes was in total rebellion against Qin officers and had reached agreement with the feudal states, and the feudal states were all leading their multitudes and heading westwards. The Governor of Pei in command of several tens of thousands of men had already butchered the defenders of Wu Pass, and got someone to go in private to Gao, but Gao was afraid that Second Generation would be angry, and that punishment would befall his own person, so he pleaded illness and did not appear at court.

Second Generation dreamt that a white tiger had bitten his left-hand outside horse and killed it, so in his anxiety and puzzlement he asked for an interpretation of the dream. 'The River Jing is an evil influence,' said the diviner. Second Generation then fasted in the Wangyi palace, intending to sacrifice to the Jing and cast four white horses into the water. And he sent a messenger to reprimand Gao over the matter of the bandits. Gao was terrified and so he secretly plotted with his son-in-law Yan Yue, Governor of Xianyang, and his younger brother Zhao Cheng. 'The Supreme One does not take any notice of remonstrances,' he said, 'but now that the matter has become serious, he intends to fix the blame on our family. I intend to remove the Supreme One, and set Prince Ziying on the throne instead. Ziying is humane and unostentatious, and the people will all take notice of what he has to say.' They got the Director of Palace Gentlemen to collaborate from inside the palace and, when he pretended there was a large force of bandits, Yan Yue was ordered to summon officers and call out troops. Yan Yue's mother was pursued and seized and installed as a hostage in Gao's residence. Gao sent Yue in command of more than 1,000 officers and men to the entrance to the hall in the Wangyi palace, where they tied up the commander of the guard, saying: 'The bandits have got in here. Why did you not stop them?' The commander of the guard said: 'Troops are stationed extremely carefully in the guard-posts surrounding the place, so how could the bandits have dared to enter the palace?' Yue then beheaded the commander of the guard and led his officers straight in, firing arrows. The palace gentlemen and eunuchs were greatly astonished. Some fled and some resisted. Those who resisted immediately died, and the dead amounted to nearly 100 men.

Then the Director of Palace Gentlemen and Yan Yue went inside together and shot at the hangings above and the curtains behind the throne. Second Generation angrily called for his courtiers, but they were all agitated and did not put up a fight. At his side there was a single eunuch who remained in attendance on him and did not dare to leave. As he entered the inner apartments, Second Generation said: 'Why did you not tell me earlier? And now it has come to this!' The eunuch said: 'It is because your servant did not dare speak that he has managed to stay alive. Had he spoken earlier, how could he have survived until now, when everyone has been put to death?' Yan Yue came forward and immediately denounced Second Generation, saying: 'You, sir, are proud and wilful. In your executions you have done away with principle. The Empire has joined together to rebel against you, and now you had better make plans for yourself.' Second Generation said: 'May the Chief Minister be seen or not?' 'No, he may not,' said Yan Yue. Second Generation said: 'I would like to get a single province and become king of it', but they would not permit it. Then he said: 'I would like to become a marquis with a fief of 10,000 households', but they would not permit it. He said: 'I would like to become one of the black-headed people together with my wife and children, just like all the other princes.' Yan Yue said: 'Your servant has received orders from the Chief Minister to punish you on behalf of the Empire; and even if you, sir, have much to say, your servant does not dare to reply.' And he signalled to his soldiers to enter. Second Generation killed himself.

Yan Yue returned and reported to Zhao Gao, who then summoned all the important officials and the princes, and he told them of the circumstances in which Second Generation was punished. 'Qin was of old a state ruled by a king,' he said, 'and it was only because the First Emperor became lord of all under Heaven that he therefore adopted the title of emperor. Now the Six States have re-established themselves and Qin territory has become smaller and smaller, so it would be improper to become an emperor with an empty title. There ought to be a king as before, for that would be appropriate.'

Then Second Generation's nephew Prince Ziying was set up as King of Qin. Second Generation was buried as a black-headed person in the Yichun gardens at Du'nan. Ziying was ordered to fast as he would have to appear at the ancestral temple to receive the royal seal. After fasting for five days Ziying plotted with his two sons, saying: 'Chief Minister Gao killed Second Generation at the Wangyi palace. Fearing that all the ministers would condemn him to death, and so pretending that he was behaving righteously, he set me on the throne. I hear that Zhao Gao has in fact made a pact with Chu to wipe out the royal family of Qin so that he may become king of the area within the passes. Now supposing I present myself at the ancestral temple after I have fasted, this person intends to kill me, taking advantage of the fact that I am in the temple. I will plead illness and not go, and the Chief Minister is bound to come here himself, and when he comes, we will kill him.' Several times Gao sent people to request Ziying's presence, but Ziying did not go, so Gao did actually go in person, saying: 'There is important business at the ancestral temple, so why does the King not go?' Ziying then stabbed Zhao Gao to death in the palace where he was fasting, and Gao's three clans were exterminated, and this was announced to Xianyang.

Ziying was King of Qin for forty-six days when the Chu commander, the Governor of Pei, smashed the Qin army and entered the Wu Pass, and then reached Bashang. He sent people to negotiate the surrender of Ziying. Ziying, having tied a rope round his neck, in a plain carriage with white horses, handing over the seal of the Son of Heaven, made his surrender beside Zhidao. The Governor of Pei then entered Xianyang, sealed the palaces, treasuries, and storehouses, and then returned to the army at Bashang. After a month or so the soldiers of the feudal states arrived, Xiang Yu being the leader of the alliance. Ziying was killed, together with the princes and other members of the royal family. Then Xiangyang was butchered and its palaces set on fire and the boys and girls who were in them made prisoner, and its treasures were looted and divided up by the feudal states. After the obliteration of Qin its territory was divided into three, called the three Qin, under the King of Yong, the King of Sai, and the King of Di. Xiang Yu, as overlord of Western Chu, was responsible for the orders dividing up the Empire among the kings and feudal lords. Qin was at last wiped out. And five years later all under Heaven was restored to order by the Han.

The Grand Historiographer says: 'Boyi, the ancestor of Qin, once achieved distinction in the time of Yao and Shun, and he received territory and had a surname conferred upon him, but during the time of the Xia and Yin his descendants became obscure and dispersed. But when Zhou declined Qin began to prosper, and established a city in the western frontier regions. From the time of

Duke Mu onwards it gradually nibbled away at the feudal states, and
the end-product was the First Emperor. The First Emperor himself
thought that his achievements surpassed those of the Five Emperors,
and his territory was more extensive than that of the Three Kings, so
he felt embarrassed to be considered on a par with them.'

*The chapter continues with an essay on the faults of Qin, which was
written, not by Sima Qian, but by the Han Confucianist Jia Yi, and
is therefore not translated. This essay is followed by some other material which is out of place here and so is not translated either.*

6

THE TREATISES

This is the section of the work which comprises treatises on matters of importance to the Government; but unfortunately, although this section of dynastic histories assumed great importance as a result of the pioneer effort of Sima Qian, in the Historical Records *some of the chapters are confused and incomplete. Furthermore, most of the eight treatises include very little about the Qin Dynasty, which is unsurprising in view of its brevity. Of the three that do I have omitted the astronomical section in spite of the high regard in which it is held by experts. The reason for this is that it was very much Sima Qian's professional concern, so the material it contains is inappropriate for the non-specialist reader. I therefore confine myself to a translation of the relevant passages in chapters 28 and 29, the former of which deals with state religious practices, and the latter with rivers and canals. The chapter on religious practices is entitled 'The Feng and Shan Sacrifices', taking its name from the two very important sacrifices that were performed by Sons of Heaven when they felt confident that their virtuous rule had fully justified their position.*

WHEN the First Emperor of Qin, having unified all under Heaven, had become emperor, someone said: 'The Yellow Emperor obtained the Power of Earth, and a yellow dragon and an earthworm appeared. The Xia obtained the Power of Wood, and a green dragon stopped at the bounds, and the grass and trees became luxuriant. The Yin obtained the Power of Metal, and silver flowed forth from the mountains. The Zhou obtained the Power of Fire, and there was the omen of the red bird.* Now that the Qin has replaced the Zhou, it is time for the Power of Water. Once upon a time, when Duke Wen of Qin sallied forth to hunt, he captured a black dragon, and this was his omen indicating the Power of Water.' Thereupon Qin renamed the Yellow River as the 'Powerful Water', and took the tenth month, which was in winter, as the beginning of the year. Among colours they gave priority to black, and they treated six as the basis for measurement, and in sounds they gave priority to *dalü*, and in the conduct of affairs they gave priority to law.

Three years after he had assumed the position of emperor, he journeyed east and toured the provinces and districts. He made a sacrifice at Mount Yi in Zou and extolled the exploits of Qin. He then summoned seventy Confucian masters and scholars of broad learning from Qi and Lu who were in attendance to come to the foot of Mount Tai. Among the various Confucian masters someone counselled that 'When the *feng* and *shan* were performed in antiquity, the carriage wheels were wrapped in rushes, for they hated to do harm to the soil or vegetation on the mountain; they sacrificed when the earth had been swept, and for mats they used rushes and grain-stalks, so the description would be easy to comply with.' The First Emperor heard the counsel of these people, but each suggestion was bizarre and difficult to adopt, and as a result he got rid of the Confucian masters.

Next he opened up a roadway for carriages and, ascending via the southern face of Mount Tai, he reached the summit, where a stone tablet was set up, extolling the virtue of the First Emperor of Qin, to make clear that he had been able to perform the *feng* sacrifice. He descended via a route on the northern side of the mountain, and made the *shan* sacrifice at Liangfu. In the ceremonies for this they drew to some extent on the procedures which had been used by the Great Supplicator when he sacrificed to the Supreme God at Yong. But the *feng* sacrifice was hidden away and kept totally secret* so that it could not be recorded by contemporaries.

When the First Emperor ascended Mount Tai, he encountered violent wind and rain when half-way up the slope, and rested beneath a huge tree. The various Confucian masters who had been dismissed, and had not been able to be present to have their advice followed with regard to the ritual adopted in the *feng* procedures, ridiculed the Emperor when they heard that he had encountered the wind and rain.

Thereupon the First Emperor next went east and travelled along the sea coast. On his journey he performed rituals and sacrificed to the famous mountains and great rivers, together with the Eight Spirits, and searched for immortals such as Xianmen.

As for the Eight Spirits, it seems that they have existed since antiquity. Some say that this worship has been carried out since the Great Duke. Since sacrifices to them were not continued without a break, nobody knows when they started. Of the Eight Spirits, the first is called the Sovereign of Heaven, and it is sacrificed to at the Navel of Heaven, which is a deep pool situated at the foot of a mountain in the southern environs of Linzi.* (The reason why Qi was called Qi is because of the Navel of Heaven.) The second is called the Sovereign of Earth and it is sacrificed to at Liangfu near Mount Tai. To be sure, since it is said that Heaven loves the Yin, sacrifices to it must take place at the foot of a high mountain or at the top of a small mountain, naming it as the 'sacred site'; and since Earth honours the Yang, offerings to it must take place on a round hill in the middle of marshy land. The third is called the Sovereign of Weapons, and one sacrificed to Chi You.* Chi You was situated in the district of Lujian in the province of Tongping, which is on the western borders of Qi. The fourth is called the Sovereign of Yin and it is sacrificed to at the Three Mountains. The fifth is called the Sovereign of Yang and it is sacrificed to at Zhifu. The sixth is called the Lord of the Moon and it is sacrificed to at Mount Lai. All of these were in the north of Qi, along the shore of Bohai. The seventh is called the Sovereign of the Sun and it is sacrificed to at Mount Cheng. Mount Cheng slopes steeply into the sea, and it is said that it is situated in the extreme north-eastern corner of Qi, to welcome the sunrise. The eighth is called the Sovereign of the Four Seasons and it is sacrificed to at Langye. Langye is in the eastern area of Qi, surely where the year begins. In each case sacrifice was offered using one set of sacrificial victims, but as to the additions and reductions introduced by the shamans and priests, as well as the jade tablets and silk offerings—these were various.

From the times of Wei and Xuan of Qi the disciples of Master Cou* discussed and wrote about the succession of the Five Powers. When Qin became an empire, the men of Qi submitted an account of this, and so the First Emperor made use of it. Song Wuji,

Zhengbo Qiao, Chong Shang, and, last of all, Xianmen Gao were all men of Qi. They practised magic and the way of the immortals, and their bodies disintegrated, melted, and were transformed, and they relied on the activities of ghosts and spirits. Cou Yan became distinguished in the feudal states because of the Yin and Yang and the succession of the Five Powers, and the magicians from the sea coast of Yan and Qi handed down his techniques but could not understand them. Consequently there developed from this a situation in which there were innumerable exponents of the bizarre but flattering and ingratiating.

From the time of Wei and Xuan and Zhao of Yan, people had been sent to sea to seek Penglai, Fangzhang, and Yingzhou. These three spirit mountains were said to be situated in the Bohai, and they were not far away from human beings; but the trouble was that when one was about to reach them, the boat would be driven off course by the wind. To be sure, there once existed people who reached these places, and both immortals and the elixir of ever-lasting life were to be found there. All the flora and fauna there were white, and the palaces and gates were made of gold and silver. Before one arrived they were like clouds as one gazed upon them from afar; but when one did get there, the three spirit mountains were situated upside-down beneath the water. As one approached them, the wind suddenly drove one off course, and it is said that in the end nobody could reach them. All the rulers of the time felt frustrated at this.

Coming to the time when the First Emperor of Qin unified all under Heaven, when he reached the sea coast innumerable magicians mentioned these places. The First Emperor considered going to sea himself, but was afraid he would not reach them, so he appointed someone to send youths and maidens to sea in search of them. Although boats passed backwards and forwards over the sea, they all made the wind their excuse and said that they had so far been unable to get there, but had seen them in the distance.

Next year the First Emperor again travelled along the sea coast, and went as far as Langye. He passed Mount Heng and returned via Shangdang. Three years later he travelled to Jieshi and interrogated the magicians who had gone to sea, and then returned home via Shang province. Five years later the First Emperor went south and reached Mount Xiang, and next he climbed Kuaiji and went along the sea coast, hoping to come across the marvellous elixirs from the three spirit mountains in the sea. He did not obtain them and, when he reached Shaqiu on his return, he passed away.*

In the first year of his reign Second Generation made a tour eastwards to Jieshi, followed the coastline southwards, went past Mount Tai, and reached Kuaiji. He performed ceremonies and sacrifices at all these places, and engraved inscriptions on the side of the writings on the stone tablets which the First Emperor had erected, in order to make manifest the achievements and virtue of the First Emperor. In the autumn of that year the feudal states rebelled against Qin, and in his third year Second Generation died by assassination.

Qin perished twelve years after the First Emperor had performed the *feng* and *shan* sacrifices. All the Confucian scholars hated Qin for burning the *Songs* and the *Documents*, and putting to death the men of letters, and the people resented its laws, so all under Heaven rebelled against it and completely misrepresented the situation by saying: 'When the First Emperor climbed Mount Tai, he was attacked by violent wind and rain and could not perform the *feng* and *shan*.' Is this not what is meant by one who performs sacrifices although he lacks the virtue for it?

In ancient times the rulers of the Three Dynasties were all to be found between the Yellow River and the Luo. Therefore Mount Song was regarded as the Central Peak, and the four peaks each corresponded with their own particular directions. The four watercourses were all east of the mountains. When Qin adopted the name of 'emperor' and the capital was established at Xianyang, the five peaks and the four watercourses were all likewise in the east. From the Five Emperors down to Qin, prosperity alternated with decay, and some of the famous mountains and great rivers were within the territory of the feudal lords and some within the territory of the Son of Heaven. The ceremonies used at these places fluctuated and varied from age to age, so they cannot be completely recorded. When Qin unified all under Heaven, orders were given that there should be a systematization of those offerings which had been regularly made by the officials responsible for sacrifices to Heaven and Earth, the famous mountains, the great rivers, and the ghosts and spirits.

After that, to the east of Xiao sacrifices were offered to five famous mountains and two great rivers. They were called the Great Room (which is Mount Song), Mount Heng, Mount Tai, Kuaiji, and Mount Xiang. The rivers were the Ji and the Huai. In spring a sacrifice was made using dried meat and wine for the sake of the harvest, and as a result the ice was made to thaw. In autumn they made the water freeze, and in winter prayers and sacrifices of thanksgiving were made. At each of these sacrifices a single offering of an ox and a calf was used, but the implements and the jade and silk were different in each case.

To the west of Hua there were seven famous mountains and four famous rivers. They were called Mount Hua, Mount Bo (alias Mount Shuai), Mount Yue, Mount Qi, Wu Peak, Crane Mound, and Mount Du (alias Mount Wen in Shu). The rivers were the Yellow River (which was sacrificed to at Linjin), the Mian (which was sacrificed to at Hanzhong), the Jiao Deep (which was sacrificed to at Chaona, and the Yangtze (which was sacrificed to at Shu).

Likewise sacrifices for thawing and freezing in spring and autumn, as well as prayers of thanksgiving, were offered, just as to the famous mountains and streams of the east. The sacrificial victims were an ox and a calf, but the implements, jades and silks, were different in each case. Also the four great peaks of Hong, Qi, Wu, and Yue all received fresh grain. The Treasures of Chen* were sacrificed to at the season when they appeared, and the Yellow River in addition had a sacrifice of newly made unstrained wine. These were all in the region of Yongzhou, near to the capital of the Son of Heaven, so a carriage and four red horses with black manes were added.

The Ba, Chan, Changshui, Feng, Lao, Jing, and Wei were all of them not great rivers, but because of their proximity to Xianyang they all got sacrifices comparable with those received by the mountains and rivers, although without the various additions. Rivers such as the Qian, Luo, Two Deeps, and Mingze, and mountains such as Mount Pu and Mount Yuexu, although they were small

rivers and mountains, were also all given prayers for the harvest and
sacrifices for thawing, freezing, and thanksgiving, although the
ritual was not necessarily the same.

*At this point a passage equivalent to about a page in translation is
omitted because it consists of a further list of places of worship and
sacrifice.*

In Qin the spirits which had only the tiniest amount of divine
power were each offered sacrifices in accordance with the season
of the year. But the supreme gods of the four sacred places at Yong
were deemed the most honourable. But it was only the Treasures
of Chen whose luminosity moved the people. Therefore in the
four sacred places at Yong in spring prayers were said for the harvest,
and because of this the ice was made to thaw, and in autumn the
waters were made to freeze, and in winter sacrifices of thanksgiving were made. In spring and summer red colts were used and in
autumn and winter red colts with black manes. In the sacred places
four colts were used, together with wooden images of one team of
four dragons drawing a belled carriage and one team of four horses
drawing an ordinary carriage, each in accordance with the colour
of the appropriate deity. Four yellow calves and four lambs, each
together with a specific number of jades and silks, were all buried
alive, and there was no paraphernalia such as stands and platters.

The sacrifice at the bounds took place once every three years.
Qin took the tenth month in winter as the beginning of the year,
and so it was always the tenth month when the Emperor fasted
and appeared at the bounds. Beacon fires were raised, and he
made his prostrations on the Xianyang side, and in his vestments
white was predominant, and it is said that his practices conformed
with those of ordinary sacrifices. The sacrifices at the western
sacred place and the sacred place of Xi conformed with their previous practice, but the Emperor did not go in person.

All these sacrifices the Great Supplicator regularly presided
over, and sacrifices were offered in accordance with the seasons of
the year. With regard to, for example, the other famous mountains
and rivers and the various ghosts and also the Eight Spirits, if the

Emperor was passing, he made a sacrifice; but when he left, it was over and done with. As for those who sacrificed to the spirits in the remote regions of the provinces and districts, in each case the people themselves offered up the sacrifices, and they were not directed by the supplicatory officials of the Son of Heaven. Among the supplicatory officials there was the Secret Supplicator. As soon as there was an omen of disaster, he immediately offered up prayers and sacrifices so that the fault might instead be visited on inferiors.

There follows a much shorter extract from the treatise on rivers and canals, which gives a fuller account of the construction of the Zheng Guo Canal which was referred to briefly in the biography of Li Si.

But Hann heard that Qin was fond of embarking on enterprises, so with the intention of causing its energies to be dissipated and in order to prevent it from making an attack to the east, it accordingly dispatched a water engineer named Zheng Guo to give controversial advice to Qin by making it excavate a canal from the Jing river west of Mount Zhong as far as Hukou, from where it was to go east along the Northern Mountains and flow into the Luo. It would be more than 300 *li* long, and the intention would be to use it to irrigate the fields. When it was half completed the true purpose was realized, and Qin intended to kill Zheng Guo, but Zheng Guo said: 'At first I was acting in order to cause dissension, but when the canal is completed it will surely be a benefit to Qin.' Qin thought this was true, so in the end had the progress on the canal continued. When the canal did make further progress, it was used to cause the stagnant waters to flow, and irrigate the salty land over an area of more than 40,000 *qing,* so that the harvest totalled one *zhong* per *mou.** Thereupon the area within the passes was turned into fertile but uncultivated land, and there were no calamitous years, and thus Qin became rich and strong, and in the end unified the feudal states. Because of this it was called the Zheng Guo Canal.

7

THE STORY OF THE REBEL XIANG YU

Xiang Yu has already been mentioned as one of the rebels who toppled the Qin Dynasty. Chapter 7 of the Historical Records *tells his story.*

A CERTAIN Xiang Ji was a man of Xiaxiang, and his courtesy name was Yu. When he first rose up in rebellion, he was 24 years old. His father's youngest brother was Xiang Liang, and Liang's father had been the Chu general Xiang Yan, who was the one whom the Qin general Wang Jian had brought to a shameful death. The Xiang family had been generals of Chu for generation after generation and had been given a fief at Xiang, and so they had been surnamed Xiang.

When Xiang Yu was young he studied writing but did not persist. Having abandoned this, he studied swordsmanship, but again did not persist. Xiang Liang lost his temper with him, so Yu said: 'Writing is useful only for recording names. With the sword one opposes a single individual, so it is not worth studying. I will study to oppose 10,000 men.' Thereupon Xiang Liang did indeed teach Yu military tactics, and although Yu was highly delighted and became aware of the meaning of the subject in outline, he again refused to pursue these studies to the limit.

Xiang Liang was once arrested at Yueyang, so he requested Cao Jiu, the prison official of Ji, to, send a letter to Sima Xin, the prison official of Yueyang, and on account of this he got let off.

Xiang Liang killed someone, so together with Yu he went to Wuzhong to escape those who would exact vengeance. The men of quality and the grandees of Wuzhong all appeared to be inferior to Xiang Liang. Every time there was a major public work in Wuzhong or a funeral, Xiang Liang was always put in charge. Less publicly he trained his friends together with the local youth in military tactics, and in these ways his abilities became known.

When the First August Emperor of Qin was at Kuaiji on tour and was being ferried across the River Zhe, Liang and Yu were watching together. 'That one could be captured and replaced,' said Yu. Liang put his hand over his mouth and said: 'Don't talk rubbish or our clan will be wiped out!'* But Liang marvelled at Yu because of this. Yu was more than 8 feet* tall and strong enough to be able to carry a big cauldron. His talent and spirit were both exceptional, and even the young men of Wuzhong had all become terrified of Yu.

In the seventh month of the first year of the Second Generation Emperor of Qin, Chen Sheng and others started an uprising in Daze. In the ninth month Tong, the Governor of Kuaiji,* said to Liang: 'All of the area west of the Yangtze is in revolt, and this is surely the time when Heaven will put an end to Qin. I have heard that, if one gets in first, one gains control of others; but if one is behindhand, one is controlled by others. I wish to send forth soldiers and appoint you, sir, and Huan Chu to take command.' At this time Huan Chu had disappeared in the marshlands. Liang said: 'Huan Chu has disappeared and nobody else knows his where-abouts. Only Yu knows it and that is all.' Accordingly Liang went outside, and warned Yu to take up position outside and wait hold-ing his sword. Liang went in again and, sitting down with the Governor, he said: 'I request to summon Yu, and make him accept your instructions to summon Huan Chu.' 'All right,' said the Governor. Liang summoned Yu inside. After a short time Liang winked at Yu. 'It may be done,' he said, and thereupon Yu immedi-ately drew his sword and decapitated the Governor. Holding the Governor's head, Xiang Liang attached his seal and seal-cord to his own belt. The retainers were greatly astonished and thrown into confusion, so almost 100 of them were struck down and killed by Yu. Throughout the whole of the government building everyone prostrated himself in terror, and nobody dared to get up again. Liang then summoned those enterprising officers whom he had previously known and proclaimed his reasons for initiating a great uprising, and next raised troops in Wuzhong. Appointing people to carry out recruitment in the subordinate districts, he got together an elite force of 8,000 men. Liang appointed the stalwarts of Wuzhong to be commanders, lieutenants, and marshals. There was one person who did not get employment, so he mentioned himself to Liang. 'On a previous occasion,' said Liang, 'I appointed you to take charge of such-and-such matters at so-and-so's funeral, but you were unable to cope, and because of this I have not given you any responsibility.' So the multitude all gave their submission. Thereupon Liang became Governor of Kuaiji and Yu became assistant-general, and all the subordinate districts were brought to submission.

A man of Guangling called Zhao Ping thereupon tried to bring about the submission of Guangling in the interest of King Chen, but he was not at all capable of subduing it. When he heard that King Chen* had been defeated and put to flight and that the Qin army was also about to arrive, he accordingly crossed the Yangtze and fabricated a command from King Chen that Liang be appointed Supreme Pillar of the State to the King of Chu. 'Now that the area east of the Yangtze has been settled,' he said, 'you should urgently lead forth your troops and march west to smite Qin.' Xiang Liang accordingly crossed the Yangtze with 8,000 men and marched west. When he heard that Chen Ying had already subdued Dongyang, he sent an emissary desiring to join forces with him so that they might go westwards together. Chen Ying had formerly been a clerk to the district magistrate of Dongyang. Because of his unfailing honesty and diligence while he was resident in the district, he was praised as a venerable person. When the district magistrate was killed by the young men of Dongyang, they formed themselves into a band of several thousand men and wished to establish a leader, and since there was no one else who answered the purpose, they accordingly invited Chen Ying. Although Ying declined on the pretext of his inability, they subsequently insisted on setting him up as their leader, and within the district he got followers to the number of 20,000. The young men wished to go further and set Ying up as king, and they started a separate rising, wearing blue caps to distinguish their forces.

Chen Ying's mother said to him: 'Ever since I came into your family as a bride I have never heard of the existence of noblemen among your ancestors. If you suddenly acquire a great name, it will be unlucky. The best thing would be if there were someone else to attach yourself to, so that if the enterprise is brought to success you may still get a fief; but if the enterprise fails it will be easy to make a getaway, since you will not be someone whose name the world points to.' So Ying did not venture to become king. 'The Xiangs are a family who have produced generals for generation after generation,' he told his officers, 'and they are renowned in Chu. If you intend to start a great enterprise, it would be improper if the general were not one of them. If we depend on a famous clan, the destruction of Qin will become inevitable.' Thereupon the multitude accepted his recommendation, and the soldiers were handed over to Xiang Liang. And when Xiang Liang crossed the Huai,* Qing Bu and General Pu also handed over their troops to him. In all 60,000 or 70,000 men encamped at, Xiapei.

Meanwhile Qin Jia had already set up Jing Ju as King of Chu and encamped to the east of Pengcheng,* intending to oppose Xiang Liang. 'King Chen was at the head of the business first of all,' said Xiang Liang to his army officers, 'but in battle he did not secure an advantage, and we have not yet heard his whereabouts. If Qin Jia ignores King Chen and sets Jing Ju on the throne, this is treacherous and unprincipled.' Accordingly he moved his troops forward and attacked Qin Jia. Qin Jia's army was defeated and put to flight, and he was pursued as far as Huling. Jia turned back and fought all day long, but he died and his army surrendered. Jing Ju fled and died in the territory of Liang. Having absorbed Qin Jia's army into his own, Xiang Liang encamped at Huling, intending to march westwards at the head of his army.

The army of Zhang Han* had reached Li, and Xiang Liang sent a detachment under the command of Zhu Jishi and Yu Fanjun to do battle with him. Yu Fanjun died and Zhu Jishi's army was defeated, but he escaped and fled to Huling. Xiang Liang accordingly led his troops into Xue and executed Jishi. Xiang Liang had previously sent Xiang Yu to make a separate attack on Xiangcheng, but Xiangcheng put up a strong defence and did not submit; so, when it was seized, it was totally laid waste. He returned and reported this to Xiang Liang. When Xiang Liang heard that King Chen was certainly dead, he summoned all the commanders of separate detachments to gather together at Xue and plan what was to be done. At this time the Governor of Pei* had also caused Pei to rise up in revolt, and he was present on this occasion.

Fan Zeng, a man of Juchao, a 70-year-old who usually stayed at home, but had a fondness for concocting bizarre plans, went and told Xiang Liang: 'Chen Sheng's defeat was certainly appropriate. When Qin destroyed the Six States, Chu was the most blameless. Ever since King Huai* entered Qin and did not return, the men of Chu have felt sorry for him right up to the present, and that is why Master Nan of Chu said: "Even if Chu consisted of only three households, if Qin is destroyed it is bound to be Chu's doing." Now since Chen Sheng, when he was in charge of the business, did not set on the throne a descendant of Chu but instead set himself up, his power did not last long. Now that you, my lord, have risen up in the east of the Yangtze, a swarm of Chu generals have all striven to join you, thinking that you, whose family have been generals of Chu from generation to generation, will be able to restore a descendant of Chu.' Thereupon, thinking his words were true, Xiang Liang consequently sought out Xin, a grandson of King Huai of Chu, who was living among the common people and working as a shepherd for somebody else, and promptly made him King Huai of Chu in accordance with what the people were hoping for. Chen Ying became Supreme Pillar of the State of Chu and was enfeoffed with five districts, and together with King Huai established a capital at Xuyi. And Xiang Liang entitled himself Lord of Wuxin.

After a few months he led his troops forth and attacked Kangfu, and together with the armies of Tian Rong of Qi and Marshal Long Qie he went to the relief of Donga, and inflicted a major defeat on the Qin army at Donga. Having led his army back home, Tian Rong drove out his king, Jia, and Jia fled to Chu while his chief minister, Tian Jue, fled to Zhao. Jue's younger brother Tian Jian, an erstwhile general of Qi, was living in Zhao and did not dare to return home. Tian Rong set up Shi, the son of Tian Dan, as King of Qi.* Having defeated the army below Donga, Xiang Liang next went in pursuit of the Qin army. He frequently sent emissaries to put pressure on the Qi troops, wishing to go westwards together with them. But Tian Rong said: 'If Chu will kill Tian Jia and Zhao will kill Tian Jue and Tian Jian, I will in fact send forth troops.' Xiang Liang said: 'Tian Jia was the king of an allied state who came and joined me in his distress so I could not bear to kill him.' Zhao also did not kill Tian Jue and Tian Jian in order to do a deal

with Qi. So Qi refused to send out troops to help Chu. Xiang Liang
sent the Governor of Pei and Xiang Yu to make a separate attack
on Chengyang and butchered it. Then they went west and defeated
the Qin army east of Puyang. The Qin soldiers gathered themselves
together and entered Puyang. Then the Governor of Pei and Xiang
Yu attacked Dingtao. When Dingtao did not submit, they withdrew
and seized territory to the west as far as Yongqiu. They inflicted
a major defeat on the Qin army and decapitated Li You.* On their
return they attacked Waihuang, but Waihuang did not submit.

Starting out from Donga, Xiang Liang went westwards and
reached Dingtao, where he again defeated a Qin army; and since
he and his followers had also decapitated Li You, Xiang Yu became
all the more contemptuous of Qin and wore an arrogant expression.
Accordingly Song Yi* reprimanded him, saying: 'If a general
becomes arrogant and his troops become idle because of a victory
in battle, then they will be defeated. Now the troops have become
a little idle, and the Qin soldiers increase in numbers day by day, and
I am fearful of this for your sake.' But Xiang Liang did not listen
to him. In fact he sent Song Yi on a mission to Qi. On the way he
encountered a Qi emissary, Xian, Lord of Gaoling. 'Are you intending to see the Lord of Wuxin?' he said. 'Yes,' he replied. 'I suggest
that the army of the Lord of Wuxin will certainly be defeated,' he
said. 'If you go slowly, then you will escape death; but if you go
quickly, then you will come upon disaster.' Qin did in fact raise all
the soldiers it could to reinforce Zhang Han, and he attacked the Chu
army and heavily defeated it at Dingtao, and Xiang Liang died.

The Governor of Pei and Xiang Yu left Waihuang and attacked
Chenliu, but Chenliu was strongly defended and they could not
subdue it. The Governor of Pei and Xiang Yu made plans together,
saying: 'Now that the army of Xiang Liang has been defeated, the
officers and soldiers are afraid.' So, together with the army of
Lü Chen, they led forth their troops and went eastwards. Lü Chen
encamped east of Pengcheng, Xiang Yu encamped west of
Pengcheng, and the Governor of Pei encamped at Dang.

When he had defeated the army of Xiang Liang, Zhang Han
considered that the soldiers of the land of Chu were not worth
worrying about, so he crossed the Yellow River and attacked Zhao,

and inflicted a major defeat upon it. At this time Zhao Xie was king, Chen Yu was general, and Zhang Er was chancellor, and they all fled to the walls of Julu.* Zhang Han ordered Wang Li and She Jian to besiege Julu, and Zhang Han himself encamped to the south of it and built a walled road to transport grain to them. Chen Yu was the general and he was in command of several tens of thousands of troops and they encamped north of Julu, and this was the so-called 'army north of the Yellow River'.

When the soldiers of Chu had been defeated at Dingtao, King Huai was afraid and went from Xuyi to Pengcheng. Combining the armies of Xiang Yu and Lü Chen, he took personal command of them. He appointed Lü Chen as minister of education, and appointed his father, Lü Qing, as chief minister. He appointed the Governor of Pei as chief of the province of Dang, and enfeoffed him as Marquis of Wuan, and he was to take command of the soldiers in the Dang province.

Before this the Qi emissary Xian Lord of Gaoling, whom Song Yi had encountered, had entered the Chu army. When he was received in audience by the King of Chu, he said: 'Song Yi argued that the army of the Lord of Wuxin would certainly be defeated, and after a few days the army was actually defeated. To see the evidence of defeat before the soldiers have gone into battle—this may be called understanding soldiers.' So the King summoned Song Yi to make a plan of action with him and was greatly pleased with him, and he therefore decided to appoint him supreme general. Xiang Yu was made Duke of Lu and became second in command, and Fan Zeng became junior general, to go to the relief of Zhao. All the generals of separate detachments were subordinated to Song Yi, whose title was Minister at the Head of the Armies.

On their march they reached Anyang, where they stayed for forty-six days and did not advance. Xiang Yu said: 'I hear that the Qin army is besieging the King of Zhao at Julu, so if we quickly lead our soldiers across the Yellow River and Chu attacks from the outside and Zhao responds from within, then the defeat of the Qin army will be inevitable.' 'Not so,' said Song Yi. 'The gadfly that attacks an ox cannot destroy the lice. If Qin attacks Zhao and is victorious in battle, then its soldiers will be exhausted, and we shall benefit from their weariness; but if they are not victorious, then we shall lead our soldiers and march westwards, sounding the drum on our journey, and we shall certainly take Qin. Therefore the best thing is to let Qin and Zhao fight first of all. At donning armour and wielding the sword, I am not the equal of you, sir; but at sitting down and turning over plans, you are not as good as me.'Accordingly he sent down orders throughout the army saying: 'Those who are as fierce as tigers, obstinate as rams, and greedy as wolves, but whose strength cannot be disciplined are all to be put to death.'

Then he sent his son Song Xiang to become Chief Minister of Qi, and personally escorted him as far as Wuyan, where he held a drinking-party for those of high rank. The weather was cold and it was raining heavily, and both officers and men were frozen and starving. Xiang Yu said: 'We shall join forces and attack Qin, for it will not do to hang about a long time. At present the harvest threatens famine and the people are poor, and officers and men feed on taro root and pulse, and there is no sign of provisions for the army, yet he is actually holding a drinking-party for the high-ups. He does not lead the soldiers across the Yellow River to take advantage of the food in Zhao to combine forces with Zhao to attack Qin, but even says: "We shall benefit from their weariness." Now when a newly created Zhao is attacked by means of the strength of Qin, its power is bound to take Zhao. If Zhao is taken and Qin is strong, what weariness is there to benefit from! Moreover, since the soldiers of our state were recently defeated, the King does not rest easy on his throne and, since he made a clean sweep within the frontiers and has subordinated everyone to the General alone, then the safety or danger of the state depends on this single enterprise. But now he does not feel sorry for his officers and men, but follows his private interests, so he is not a true servant of the altars of the land and grain.'

That morning, when Xiang Yu paid a formal visit to the supreme general, Song Yi, he cut off Song Yi's head within his tent, and sent out orders throughout the army saying: 'Song Yi plotted with Qi to revolt against Chu, and the King of Chu secretly ordered me to put him to death.' At this time all the generals submitted in terror, and nobody dared to put up any resistance. They all said: 'It was the general's family that was at the forefront in establishing

Chu, and now the general is punishing treachery.' So they got together and jointly set up Xiang Yu as acting supreme general. People were sent to pursue Song Yi's son, and when they reached Qi he was killed. Huan Chu was sent to make a report to King Huai and receive instructions from him. King Huai accordingly appointed Xiang Yu to be supreme general, and Qing Bu and General Pu both placed themselves under Xiang Yu.

Having killed the Minister at the Head of the Armies, Xiang Yu inspired awe in the state of Chu and became famous throughout the feudal states. Accordingly he dispatched Qing Bu and General Pu in command of 20,000 troops to cross the Yellow River, and go to the relief of Julu. They gained little advantage in the fighting and Chen Yu again requested soldiers. So Xiang Yu led all the soldiers across the Yellow River. He sank all the boats, smashed the pots and pans, and set fire to the huts, and kept only three days' supplies in order to demonstrate to his officers and men that they must die and not have a single thought of returning. So when they arrived, they surrounded Wang Li and encountered the Qin army. After nine battles they had breached their walled roadway, inflicted a major defeat upon them, killed Su Jue, and taken Wang Li prisoner. She Jian did not surrender to Chu but burnt himself to death.

At this time the soldiers of Chu* capped those of the feudal states. There were more than ten walled camps nearby occupied by armies of the feudal states which had gone to the relief of Julu, but nobody had dared to commit his soldiers. When Chu attacked Qin, the generals all looked on from the top of their ramparts. It only took one of the fighting men of Chu to stand up to ten of their adversaries, and the shouts of the Chu soldiers moved Heaven, and not a single person in the armies of the feudal states was not terrified. And so when he had defeated the Qin army, Xiang Yu summoned to interview the generals of the feudal states, and as they entered the carriage-shaft gates,* they all went forward on their knees, and nobody dared to look up at him. From this moment Xiang Yu became for the first time supreme general of the feudal states, and the feudal states were all subordinated to him.

Zhang Han made his camp at Jiyuan and Xiang Yu made his camp south of the Zhang. They contained each other but had not yet fought a battle. Since the Qin army had been repulsed on several occasions, Second Generation sent someone to reprimand Zhang Han. Zhang Han was afraid so he sent his senior scribe Xin to ask what to do. When he reached Xianyang, he waited three days at the palace gate but Zhao Gao did not give him an interview and felt suspicious. The senior scribe Xin was afraid and fled back to his camp. He did not dare to leave via the road he had formerly taken, so when Zhao Gao actually sent someone in pursuit of him, he did not catch up with him. When Xin reached the army he reported: 'Zhao Gao is in control of whatever happens within the palace and his subordinates do not have responsibility. If we fight now and are able to win victory, Gao is bound to be bitterly jealous of our success; but if we fight and are unable to win victory, we will not escape from death. I would like you, general, to give this your mature consideration.'

Chen Yu also sent a letter to Zhang Han. 'Bai Qi was a Qin general,'* it said, 'who marched south and subjugated Yan and Ying, and marched north and obliterated Mafu. The cities he attacked and the territory he seized are incalculable, but in the end he had death bestowed upon him. Meng Tian was a general of Qin, and in the north he drove back the Rong barbarians and opened up several thousand *li* of the territory of Yuzhong, but in the end he had his head cut off at Yangzhou. Why is that? Their successes were so many that Qin could not fully reward them with fiefs, and therefore it had recourse to the law and put them to death. Now you, general, have been the Qin commander for three years, and those you have lost may be counted by the hundred thousand, while the feudal states have also risen up in rebellion in ever-increasing numbers. The constant flattery of that person Zhao Gao has been going on for a long time, so now that the situation has become critical, he is consequently afraid that Second Generation will put him to death. That is why he intends to put you, general, to death on some legal pretext in order to block criticism, and to have someone replace you in order to avoid suffering calamity himself. You, general, have dwelt away from the capital for a long time, and there are many grudges against you within it, so you will be put to death whether you are successful or not. Moreover the fact that

Heaven is destroying Qin is known by everybody, no matter whether they are stupid or wise. If you, general, cannot offer outspoken remonstrance within the capital, and outside it have become the general of a ruined state, surely it is pathetic to stand out alone and wish to go on surviving! Why do you not make your soldiers retreat and form a north–south alliance with the feudal states, agreeing to make a joint attack on Qin and divide up its territories and rule them as kings, turning your faces to the south and adopting the title of "solitary one"?* This would surely be better than offering your body to be cut in two and your wife and children to be put to death?'

Zhang Han was suspicious, but he secretly sent Shi Cheng on a mission to Xiang Yu and intended to make a pact. But before this pact had been completed, Xiang Yu made General Pu lead troops day and night across the Sanhu to encamp south of the Zhang, and they fought battles with Qin and twice defeated them. Xiang Yu led all his troops and smote the Qin army on the River Yu, and inflicted a major defeat on them.

Zhang Han sent someone to see Xiang Yu, intending to make a pact. Xiang Yu summoned the army officers and took counsel with them. 'Provisions are scarce, and I intend to listen to what he has to say about a pact,' he said. 'Good,' said all the army officers. Xiang Yu accordingly arranged a meeting with him at the waste of Yin,* south of the River Yuan. Having made a treaty, Zhang Han went to see Xiang Yu and, letting the tears flow, gave him an account of Zhao Gao. Xiang Yu accordingly set Zhang Han up as King of Yong and established him in the Chu army. He appointed senior scribe Xin as supreme general, to command the Qin armies,* which would form the advance columns.

They came to Xin'an. At various times in the past when the officers or the troops of the feudal states had passed through Qin on corvée duty or on their way to guard the frontier, the officers and troops of Qin had generally treated them unceremoniously. Now when the Qin army surrendered to the feudal states, the officers and troops of the feudal states generally took advantage of their victory to employ them as slaves or captives, and readily humiliated the officers and troops of Qin. Many of the officers and troops of Qin were saying on the quiet: 'General Zhang and the rest tricked us into becoming subordinate to the feudal states, and now if we can enter the passes and defeat Qin, it will be splendid; but if we cannot, the feudal states will march east, making captives of us who are subordinate to them, and Qin will certainly put to death all our fathers, mothers, wives, and children.' The various generals got wind of their deliberations, and reported them to Xiang Yu. Xiang Yu accordingly summoned Qing Bu and General Pu. 'The officers and troops of Qin are still numerous,' he said, forming a plan. 'If they do not submit in their hearts and do not obey when we are within the passes, the situation will certainly become dangerous. The best thing would be to attack and kill them, so that we enter Qin with only Zhang Han, senior scribe Xin, and Commandant Yi.' Thereupon the Chu army made a night attack and annihilated more than 200,000 Qin troops south of the city of Xin'an.

As they marched on, they captured and assumed control over Qin territory. There were soldiers on guard in the Hangu Pass, so they were not able to enter. News was also received that the Governor of Pei had already taken Xianyang, so Xiang Yu was furious and ordered Qing Bu and others to attack the pass. Xiang Yu then went through and reached the west of the Xi. The Governor of Pei was encamped at Bashang, but he and Xiang Yu were not yet in view of each other. Cao Wushang, the marshal of the left to the Governor of Pei, sent someone to say to Xiang Yu: 'The Governor of Pei intends to reign as king over the area within the passes and to employ Ziying* as chief minister, and the treasures are all in his possession.' Xiang Yu was furious. 'Tomorrow morning', he said, 'I will feast my officers and men for them to smite and defeat the army of the Governor of Pei!' At this time Xiang Yu had soldiers to the number of 400,000 at Hongmen near Xinfeng, and the Governor of Pei had 100,000 at Bashang. Fan Zeng said to Xiang Yu: 'When the Governor of Pei resided east of the mountains, he was greedy for property and fond of attractive women, but now he has entered the passes, there are no possessions which he takes and there are no women he favours with his presence. This is because his ambition is not centred on the trivial. I have instructed people to gaze upon his vapours, and they have all become dragons and tigers in all the five colours, and these are the vapours of a Son of Heaven. Strike quickly and do not lose this opportunity.'

Xiang Bo, the Chu commander of the left was an uncle of Xiang Yu, and he was a constant admirer of Zhang Liang, Marquis of Liu. At this time Zhang Liang was a follower of the Governor of Pei, so Xiang Bo drove off by night and went to the army of the Governor of Pei to see Zhang Liang privately and tell him everything that had been going on, intending to call on Zhang Liang to go off together with him. 'Do not follow him or you will die together with him,' he said. 'I am escorting the Governor of Pei for the sake of the King of Hann,' said Zhang Liang, 'and if there is a crisis in the affairs of the Governor of Pei, it would be improper to desert, and I cannot but tell him.' So Liang went in and reported everything to the Governor of Pei. The Governor of Pei was astonished. 'What shall I do about it?' he said. 'Who formed this plan for the Great King?'* said Zhang Liang. He said: 'Some poor fish told me: "Put up a resistance at the passes and do not let the feudal states come inside, and the territory of Qin can all be reigned over." So I listened to him.' Liang said: 'Do you reckon that the Great King's officers and men are sufficient to provide a match for King Xiang?' The Governor of Pei fell silent. 'They are certainly not as good,' he said, 'so what shall I do about it?' 'I beg to go and have a word with Xiang Bo,' said Zhang Liang, 'and say that the Governor of Pei does not dare to turn his back on King Xiang.' The Governor of Pei said: 'How is it that you are friends with Xiang Bo?' 'In Qin times he used to go around with me,' he said, 'and when Xiang Bo killed someone, I saved his life. Now that we are in a critical situation, he has therefore done me the favour of coming to tell me.' 'Which of you is the elder?' said the Governor of Pei. 'He is older than me,' said Liang. 'Call him in for me,' said the Governor of Pei, 'and I will be able to serve him as if he were an elder brother.' Zhang Liang went outside and asked for Xiang Bo. Xiang Bo immediately went in and presented himself to the Governor of Pei. The Governor of Pei raised a cup of wine to toast him, and agreed to form a marriage relationship, saying: 'When I entered the passes, I did not presume to take possession of the tiniest thing I came upon. I registered the officials and people, I sealed up the treasuries, and I waited for the general. The reason why I sent generals to guard the passes was to make preparations against other brigands going in and out and doing things which were contrary to the normal practice. Day and night I was expecting the general to arrive, so how would I dare go against him! I would like you, Bo, fully to inform him that his servant would not dare to ignore his kindness.' Xiang Bo agreed. 'Tomorrow you must yourself come early and apologize to King Xiang,' he said to the Governor of Pei. 'All right,' said the Governor of Pei. At that Xiang Bo again left by night, and when he reached the army he reported all the Governor of Pei's remarks to King Xiang. Taking advantage of these remarks, he said: 'If the Governor of Pei had not first conquered the area within the passes, how would you, sir, have dared to enter? Now if someone has done one an important service, it is improper to strike him, and the best thing would be to deal with him on a friendly basis.' King Xiang agreed.

On the following day the Governor of Pei and an escort of more than 100 horsemen came to see King Xiang, and when they reached Hongmen, he apologized, saying: 'You and I, general, exerted our strength to attack Qin, with you, general, fighting to the north of the Yellow River and me fighting to the south of the Yellow River, but I did not think that I myself could be the first to enter the pass and defeat Qin, and that I would manage to see you again here. But now there have been the remarks of a petty fellow, and these have caused there to be a rift between you, general, and me.' King Xiang said: 'This your marshal of the left, Cao Wushang, said; otherwise how would I have gone so far as this?'

So on the same day King Xiang entertained the Governor of Pei and drank with him. King Xiang and Xiang Bo sat facing east, and Yafu sat facing south. (Yafu was Fan Zeng.) The Governor of Pei sat facing north. Zhang Liang was in attendance facing west. Fan Zeng frequently eyed King Xiang and three times raised the jade ornaments that he wore on his belt in order to signal to him, but King Xiang remained silent and did not respond. Fan Zeng rose and went outside to summon Xiang Zhuang.* 'Our king', he said, 'is too kind-hearted, so you go in and toast him, and when the toasting is finished, request to do a sword-dance, and take this opportunity to strike the Governor of Pei as he is seated, and kill him. If you do not do so, then you and your associates will all become prisoners.'

So Zhuang entered and toasted him. When the toasting was finished, he said: 'When our king drinks with the Governor of Pei, there is no means of providing entertainment in the camp, so I request to do a sword-dance.' 'All right,' said King Xiang. Xiang Zhuang drew his sword and rose to dance, and Xiang Bo also drew his sword and rose to dance, continually protecting the Governor of Pei with his body, so that Zhuang could not strike.

Thereupon Zhang Liang went to the gate of the camp, where he saw Fan Kuai. 'What about today's business?' said Fan Kuai. 'It is very serious,' said Liang. 'Just now Xiang Zhuang drew his sword and he is dancing, with his thoughts constantly on the Governor of Pei.' 'This has become critical,' said Kuai. 'I beg to go in and share his fate with him.' Kuai immediately girded on his sword and, carrying his shield, entered the gate of the camp. The sentries with crossed halberds wanted to prevent him from coming inside, but Fan Kuai moved his shield from side to side so as to strike them, and the sentries fell to the ground. Kuai then entered and, opening the curtain, took up a position facing west, and looked at King Xiang with a glare. His hair stood on end and his eyes opened wide.

King Xiang put his hand on his sword and rose to his knees. 'Who is our guest?' he said. 'This is Fan Kuai, the right-hand man in the Governor of Pei's chariot,' said Zhang Liang. 'A sturdy fellow,' said King Xiang. 'Bestow upon him a cup of wine.' So he was given a large cup of wine. Kuai bowed and thanked him. When he got up, he drank it as he stood there. 'Bestow on him a shoulder of pork,' said King Xiang, and then he was given a whole raw shoulder of pork. Fan Kuai laid his shield face down on the ground and, putting the shoulder of pork on it, drew his sword, cut it up, and ate it. 'Sturdy fellow, can you drink again?' said King Xiang. 'Death I will not avoid,' said Fan Kuai, 'so why should a cup of wine be worth refusing? That King of Qin* has the heart of a tiger or a wolf, and he kills people as if he cannot manage them all, punishes people as if he is afraid he may not do the lot, and all under Heaven is in revolt against him. King Huai made a pact with all the generals that "Whoever first defeated Qin and entered Xianyang would be king over it." Now the Governor of Pei was the first to defeat Qin and enter Xianyang, but he did not presume to take possession of the tiniest thing he came across, sealed the palaces and dwellings, and returned his army to Bashang, in order to wait for the Great King to arrive. That is why he sent generals to guard the passes to take precautions against other brigands going in and out and doing what is contrary to normal practice. After toil so bitter and achievements so lofty and with no reward of a fiefdom, instead you pay attention to trivial gossip and intend to put to death a man of achievements. This is simply to prolong a ruined Qin. I make so bold as to say that I will not accept this on the Great King's behalf.' Having no reply, King Xiang told him to sit down. Fan Kuai sat down beside Liang. After they had been seated for a short while, the Governor of Pei got up to go to the toilet, taking the opportunity to invite Fan Kuai to go outside too.

When the Governor of Pei had gone outside, King Xiang sent the commandant Chen Ping to summon him. 'When I went outside just now,' said the Governor of Pei, 'I never made my excuses, so what should I do about it?' Fan Kuai said: 'In an important enterprise one does not deal with trivial concerns, and in important ceremonies one does not give utterance to petty politenesses. At present it is others who have just played the part of knives and meat-stands, but we play the part of the fish and the meat, so why make one's excuses?' and so at that he left, but he ordered Zhang Liang to stay and make excuses for him.

'What were you carrying when you came here, O Great King?' asked Liang. 'I was holding a pair of white jade rings,' he said, 'intending to present them to King Xiang, and a pair of jade cups, intending to give them to Yafu, but when it so happened that they became angry, I did not venture to present them. Present them for me, sir.' 'I respectfully consent,' said Zhang Liang.

At this time King Xiang was encamped below Hongmen and the Governor of Pei was encamped at Bashang, and they were 40 *li* apart from each other. As for the Governor of Pei, he left his chariots and horsemen and slipped away, riding off alone apart from the four men, Fan Kuai, Xiahou Ying, Jin Qiang, and Ji Xin. They went on foot, carrying their swords and shields, going via the base of Mount Li and making their way through Zhiyang. 'If we follow this path,' said the Governor of Pei to Zhang Liang, 'we shall reach my army in only 20 *li*. You, sir, are to go in when you calculate that we have reached the army.' When the Governor of Pei had left and had reached the army via this route, Zhang Liang entered and apologized, saying: 'The Governor of Pei was the worse for drink so he was not able to make his excuses. He respectfully sends your servant Liang, bearing a pair of white jade rings which, bowing twice, he presents at the Great King's feet; and a pair of jade cups which, bowing twice, he offers at the feet of the supreme general.' 'Where is the Governor of Pei?' said King Xiang. Liang said: 'He heard that the Great King had a mind to reprove him for his errors, so he slipped away on his own, and has already reached the army.' For his part King Xiang accepted the rings and put them down on his seat, but Fan Zeng, having accepted the jade cups, put them down on the ground. Drawing his sword, he smashed them with a blow, saying: 'Alas, the fool is not worth plotting with. It is certainly the Governor of Pei who is the one who deprives King Xiang of empire. Our dependants have even now become prisoners because of him.' When the Governor of Pei reached the army, he immediately put Cao Wushang to death.

After a few days Xiang Yu led his soldiers forth and they went westwards and butchered Xianyang. They killed Ziying, the King of Qin who had surrendered, and they set light to the Qin palaces, and the fire was not put out for three months.* They went east, having collected the goods and valuables and women from there. Someone advised King Xiang: 'The area within the passes is blocked by mountains and rivers which form a barrier on all sides, and the territory is fertile; so it is a suitable place in which to establish a capital city in order to rule as paramount prince.' But King Xiang saw that the palaces of Qin had all been destroyed by fire, and he also cherished in his heart the desire to return home east. 'If riches and honours are not taken back to one's place of origin,' he said, 'it is like going out at night wearing embroideries, for who is there who will know about it?' The person who gave the advice said: 'People say that the men of Chu are only monkeys with caps on, and it's quite true.' When King Xiang heard this, he had the man who gave the advice immersed in boiling water.

King Xiang sent someone to fetch orders from King Huai. 'It will be just as we agreed,' said King Huai. So he honoured King Huai as the Righteous Emperor. Intending to make himself a king,*

King Xiang first of all made all the generals and ministers into kings. 'When the troubles first broke out in the Empire,' he said, 'the descendants of the rulers of the feudal states were provisionally set up in order to attack Qin. But as for those who put on their armour and wielded their swords and were at the forefront of activities, those who exposed themselves to sun and dew in the wilderness for three years so as to destroy Qin and settle all under Heaven—this is due to the efforts of the generals, ministers, and various lords as well as myself. Even though the Righteous Emperor has had no success, we certainly ought to allocate some territory for him to rule over.' The generals all approved, so the Empire was divided up* and all the generals were set up as marquises and kings.

King Xiang and Fan Zeng suspected that the Governor of Pei had really gained possession of the Empire and that matters were already amicably settled, but they also hated to turn their backs on the compact and were afraid that the feudal states would rebel against them. So they secretly plotted together, saying that 'The routes through Ba and Shu are hazardous, and people whom Qin deported all went to live in Shu.' Accordingly they announced that 'Ba and Shu are also territories within the passes.' Therefore they set up the Governor of Pei as King of Han, to reign over Ba, Shu, and Hanzhong, and establish a capital at Nanzheng. And the territory within the passes was divided into three, and the surrendered generals of Qin were made kings in order to place an obstacle in the way of the King of Han. King Xiang then set up Zhang Han as King of Yong, to reign over the area to the west of Xianyang, establishing his capital at Feiqiu.

I now omit a passage concerned mainly with the details of the allocation of kingdoms and marquisates to Xiang Yu's supporters, but conclude with Sima's account of the last few years of Xiang Yu's life. The Han Dynasty reckoned its beginning from the date of its founder's establishment as the King of Han, which has just been mentioned, but as these pages will show, the rebellion was far from being settled in his favour.

Next, in winter in the second year of the Han, Xiang Yu went north and came to Chengyang, and Tian Rong also took command of his troops and met him and fought a battle with him. Tian Rong was not victorious, so he fled as far as Pingyuan, and the people of Pingyuan killed him. Next he went north and burnt and razed the city walls and dwellings of Qi, and put to death all the surrendered troops of Tian Rong, and tied up and made captive the old and young and the womenfolk. He occupied Qi as far as the northern sea, and wreaked havoc over much of it. But the people of Qi gathered themselves together to rebel against him. Thereupon Tian Rong's younger brother Tian Heng rallied the troops of Qi who had deserted and got together a force of some ten thousands of men, and staged a rebellion at Chengyang. King Xiang was kept there because of this, but although he continued to fight he could not defeat them at all.

In spring the King of Han, having under his control the soldiers of five of the feudal states, a force of 560,000 men in all, went east and attacked Chu. When King Xiang heard about this, he ordered all the generals to attack Qi, but himself went south with 30,000 élite soldiers, and going via Lu, came out at Huling. In the fourth month all the Han forces had already entered Pengcheng and removed valuables and beautiful women from it, and every day wine was set out and a party held for those of high rank. So King Xiang came west via Xiao and attacked the Han army at dawn, and then went east and reached Pengcheng. During the day he inflicted a major defeat on the Han army. The Han army all fled, following each other into the Gu and Si Rivers, and more than 100,000 Han troops were killed. The Han troops all fled south to the mountains, and Chu also pursued and attacked them as far as east of Lingbi, on the banks of the Sui River. So when the Han army was repelled it came under pressure from Chu. Many were killed and more than 100,000 of the Han troops all went into the Sui River, which ceased to flow because of this.

The King of Han was encircled by a body of men three deep. Thereupon a great wind arose from the north-west. It felled trees, demolished houses, and raised a sandstorm. It was so gloomy that the day was like night. When this hit the Chu army, it was thrown into great confusion; and since its ranks were in disorder, the King of Han managed to make a getaway with twenty or thirty horsemen.

He intended to visit Pei and go west after collecting his family, but Chu had also sent men to pursue him to Pei, and take the King of Han's family; but they had all disappeared, so they and the King of Han did not see each other. But on the way the King of Han met up with the Emperor Hui and Yuan of Lu,* so he put them in the carriage and continued his journey. But the Chu horsemen were pursuing the King of Han, so in his desperation he pushed the Emperor Hui and Yuan of Lu out of the carriage. Every time this happened Lord Deng got down from the carriage, picked them up, and put them back on board. When this had happened three times, he said: 'Even if you are desperate, it is impossible to get on any quicker, so why get rid of them?' After that he was able to make his escape. He sought the Supreme Duke and the Empress Lü,* but they did not encounter each other. They had gone off in disguise with Shen Yiqi in attendance, and had been searching for the King of Han, but instead had met the Chu army. Then the Chu army returned with them and made a report to King Xiang, and King Xiang always kept them within the camp.

At this time the Marquis of Zhoulü, the elder brother of the Empress Lü, was stationed at Xiayi in command of troops acting on behalf of the Han. The King of Han went off in disguise and joined them, and gradually gathered together his own officers and men. He went on to Xingyang, where there was a rendezvous of all the defeated armies, and Xiao He* also sent there all the old men and young men who had not yet been conscripted from within the passes, so that it again became a formidable force. Starting out from Pengcheng, Chu drove constantly northwards, taking advantage of its victory, and fought with Han between Jing and Suo to the south of Xingyang. Han defeated Chu, so Chu was not able to get past Xingyang and go west.

When King Xiang was going to the relief of Pengcheng and pursuing the King of Han as far as Xingyang, Tian Heng also managed to rally Qi and set up Guang, the son of Tian Rong, as King of Qi. When the King of Han was defeated at Pengcheng, the feudal states all joined Chu again and turned their backs on Han. When Han based itself at Xingyang, it built a covered way connecting it with the Yellow River in order to obtain grain from the Ao Granary.*

In the third year of Han, King Xiang made several attacks so as to deprive Han of the use of the covered way. Frightened because the food was running short, the King of Han requested peace, with the area to the west of Xingyang being detached as Han territory. King Xiang wanted to listen to him but Fan Zeng, Marquis of Liyang, said: 'Han is easy to get along with, but if you let them go and do not seize them now, later on you are bound to regret it.' So King Xiang, together with Fan Zeng, urgently laid siege to Xingyang. The King of Han was worried about this, so, taking the advice of Chen Ping, he gave King Xiang cause for antagonism. When a messenger came from King Xiang, a sacrificial ox was prepared, as if the intention were to hand it to him. But when they saw the messenger, they feigned astonishment and said: 'We thought it was a messenger from Fan Zeng, but on the contrary you are a messenger from King Xiang.' So it was taken away and some poor food was given to the messenger of King Xiang to eat. When the messenger returned and made his report to King Xiang, King Xiang consequently suspected that there was collusion between Fan Zeng and Han, and gradually deprived him of authority. 'The Empire's affairs are mainly settled,' said Fan Zeng in a great rage. 'Your Majesty should manage them himself. I should like to be granted my freedom to return to the ranks.' King Xiang agreed to this, but before he had reached Pengcheng on his journey he died from an ulcerous growth which had appeared on his back.

The Han general Ji Xin advised the King of Han. 'The situation has become desperate,' he said. 'For Your Majesty's sake I beg to deceive Chu by playing the part of king, and Your Majesty may then make a secret getaway.' The King of Han thereupon sent out at night by the eastern gate of Xingyang 2,000 women clad in armour, and the Chu soldiers attacked them on all four sides. Ji Xin then mounted the yellow-canopied carriage* with its plumes attached to the left. 'The food in the city is all used up,' he said. 'So the King of Han surrenders.' While the Chu army all proclaimed their congratulations, the King of Han was also leaving via the western gate of the city together with twenty or thirty horsemen, fleeing to Chenggao. When King Xiang interviewed Ji Xin, he asked him where the King of Han was. He told him that the King of Han had escaped, so King Xiang had Ji Xin burnt to death.

The King of Han appointed the Imperial Secretary Zhou Ke, the Honourable Cong, and Wei Bao to keep guard over Xingyang. Zhou Ke and the Honourable Cong plotted together. 'It will be difficult to keep guard over a city together with the king of a state which has been made to revolt,' they said. So they collaborated to kill Wei Bao.* Chu defeated the city of Xingyang and took Zhou Ke alive. 'If you will become a commander for me,' said King Xiang to Zhou Ke, 'I will make you supreme general and enfeoff you with 30,000 households.' But Zhou Ke cursed and said: 'If you do not make haste to surrender to Han, Han will take you prisoner at this moment. You are not a match for Han.' King Xiang was angry and he boiled Zhou Ke alive, and at the same time killed the Honourable Cong.

When the King of Han left Xingyang, he fled south to Yuan and She and got hold of Bu, King of Jiujiang. Recruiting soldiers on his journey, he again entered and provided protection for Chenggao.

In the fourth year of Han, King Xiang advanced his soldiers and laid siege to Chenggao. The King of Han escaped and, accompanied only by the Honourable Teng, went out of the northern gate of Chenggao, crossed the Yellow River, and fled to Xiuwu, where he joined the armies of Zhang Er and Han Xin. The various generals gradually managed to get out of Chenggao and join the King of Han. Chu next took Chenggao and intended to go west. But Han sent soldiers to oppose them at Gong and cause them to be unable to go west.

At this time Peng Yue crossed the Yellow River and attacked Chu at Donga and killed the Chu general, the Honourable Xue. So King Xiang himself went east and attacked Peng Yue. The King of Han, having obtained command of the soldiers of the Marquis of Huaiyin, intended to cross the Yellow River and go south. But when Zheng Zhong gave the King of Han some advice, he accordingly stopped and built fortifications in Henei. He made Liu Jia take command of soldiers to go to the assistance of Peng Yue and burn the stores of Chu. King Xiang went east and attacked and defeated them and caused Peng Yue to flee. As for the King of Han, he led his soldiers across the Yellow River, retook Chenggao, and made camp at Guangwu, where they fetched food from the

Ao Granary. King Xiang, having pacified the eastern coastal area, came west and pitched camp facing Guangwu, just like the Han. They kept watch on each other for several months.

Meanwhile Peng Yue caused several rebellions in Liang territory and cut off Chu provisions. King Xiang was worried about this. He constructed a high sacrificial stand and placed the Supreme Duke on it and announced to the King of Han: 'If you do not submit quickly, I shall boil the Supreme Duke.' The King of Han said: 'When you, Xiang Yu, and I together faced north to receive our commands from King Huai, we said that we made a pact to become brothers, so my father is your father. If you must insist on boiling your own father, then do me the honour of allotting me a cup of soup.' King Xiang was angry and intended to kill him, but Xiang Bo said: 'What will happen to the Empire cannot yet be known about, and moreover one who runs the Empire pays no heed to his family, so even if you kill him, there will be no benefit. You will only be increasing your misfortunes, that is all.' King Xiang followed his advice.

Chu and Han held each other in check for a long time and the outcome remained indecisive. The able-bodied men suffered the hardships of military life, and the old and the young grew weary from transporting provisions by land and water. King Xiang said to the King of Han: 'That all under Heaven has been in chaos for several years now is due only to the two of us, so I would like to challenge you to single combat to decide who is cock and hen, for the sake of not bringing hardship to the fathers and sons among the people of all under Heaven.' The King of Han made his excuses with a smile. 'I would rather compete in wisdom,' he said, 'since I cannot compete in strength.'

King Xiang then ordered a valiant fellow to go forth and make a challenge to single combat. Han had an excellent mounted archer known as Lou Fan. Chu challenged him to combat three times, but Lou Fan immediately shot and killed his adversary. King Xiang was furious, so he himself put on his armour and brandished his spear and made a challenge to single combat. Lou Fan intended to shoot him, but King Xiang glared and shouted at him, so Lou Fan did not dare to look him in the eye or raise his hand, and he ran off back inside the ramparts and did not dare emerge again. The King of Han sent someone to ask questions about him on the quiet, and when it turned out that it was King Xiang, the King of Han was astonished. After that King Xiang actually approached the King of Han and they held conversation with each other facing across the gorge of Guangwu. When the King of Han reprimanded him, King Xiang became angry, and wanted to fight him in single combat. The King of Han did not take any notice, so King Xiang shot and hit him with a concealed crossbow. The King of Han was wounded and fled into Chenggao.

When King Xiang heard that the Marquis of Huaiyin had taken Hebei, had defeated Qi and Zhao, and moreover was intent on smiting Chu, he accordingly sent Long Ju to go and smite him. The Marquis of Huaiyin fought a battle with him, and Cavalry General Guan Ying smote him, inflicted a major defeat on the Chu army, and killed Long Ju. The Marquis of Huaiyin availed himself of this opportunity to set himself up as King of Qi. When King Xiang heard that Long Ju's army had been defeated, he became afraid and sent Wu She, a man of Xuyi, to go and speak to the Marquis of Huaiyin. The Marquis of Huaiyin did not take any notice of him.

At this time Peng Yue again rebelled and caused the territory of Liang to submit, and cut off grain from Chu. So King Xiang spoke to the Marquis of Haichun, Grand Marshal Cao Jiu, and others. 'If you carefully protect Chenggao,' he said, 'then if Han desires to challenge you to battle, be careful not to fight with him, and do not enable him to go east, that is all. In fifteen days I will certainly punish Peng Yue, settle the territory of Liang, and return and join you.' So he went east and *en route* attacked Chenliu and Waihuang.

Waihuang did not capitulate, but fell after a few days. King Xiang was angry and ordered all the young men over the age of 15 to come to the east of the city, for he intended to annihilate them. The 13-year-old son of the steward of the Governor of Waihuang went and spoke to King Xiang. 'Peng Yue oppressed Waihuang so powerfully that Waihuang was terrified and was consequently on the point of submission and was waiting for Your Majesty. But now that Your Majesty has arrived, if you then annihilate them, surely none of the people will turn their hearts towards you? To the east of here there are more than ten cities of the territory of Liang and they are all afraid, so none will be willing to submit.' King Xiang thought that what he said was true, so he pardoned the people of Waihuang who were due to be annihilated. Then he went east and reached Suiyang. Hearing about this, everyone strove to submit to King Xiang.

Han actually challenged the Chu army several times to battle, but the Chu army did not sally forth. He sent men to insult them for five or six days and the grand marshal grew angry and made his soldiers cross the Si River. When the officers and men were half across, Han attacked them and inflicted a major defeat on the Chu army, and seized all the valuables of the state of Chu. Grand Marshal Cao Jiu, the chief scribe Tong Yi, and Sima Xin King of Sai all cut their throats on the bank of the River Si. (Grand Marshal Jiu had formerly been prison official of Ji and senior scribe Xin had also formerly been prison officer of Yueyang, and both men had once done Xiang Liang a favour,* and therefore King Xiang had trusted them and given them responsibility.) Meanwhile King Xiang was in Suiyang, and when he heard that the army of the Marquis of Haichun had been defeated, he led forth his army and returned. The Han army had just laid siege to Zhonglimo to the east of Xingyang but, when King Xiang arrived, the Han army, through fear of Chu, had all fled to difficult terrain.

At this time the Han soldiers were flourishing and their food was plentiful, but King Xiang's soldiers were weary and their food was depleted. Han sent Lu Jia to parley with King Xiang. He asked for the Supreme Duke, but King Xiang did not take any notice of him. The King of Han next sent the Honourable Hou to go and parley with King Xiang, so King Xiang made a pact with Han* to divide up all under Heaven, with the area to the west of the Hong Canal to be separated off as Han and the area to the east of the Hong Canal to be Chu. When King Xiang had agreed to this, he restored the King of Han's father, mother, and wife, and the army all cried out 'Long life!' The King of Han then enfeoffed the Honourable Hou as 'the Lord who has pacified the State'. He retired and refused to see them again. (It was said that he was the most outstanding debater in the world and that wherever he resided he overturned the state, and so he was called 'the Lord who has pacified the State'.)* After he had concluded the pact, King Xiang led his soldiers away, released them, and returned east.

Han intended to return to the west, but Zhang Liang and Chen Ping said: 'Han has possession of the greater part of all under Heaven, and the feudal lords are all dependent on it. The Chu soldiers are weary and their food is all used up, so this is the time when Heaven is destroying Chu. The best thing would be to take advantage of such an opportunity and go on to seize it. If you let it get away now and do not attack it, this is what is called "leaving oneself worries by feeding a tiger".' The King of Han paid attention to them.

Accordingly in the fifth year of Han the King of Han pursued King Xiang to the south of Yangxia, where he halted his army. Then he fixed a rendezvous with Han Xin, Marquis of Huaiyin, and Peng Yue, Marquis of Jiancheng, to attack the Chu army. But when he reached Guling the armies of Han Xin and Peng Yue were not there to meet him and Chu attacked the Han army and inflicted a major defeat on them. The King of Han went back inside his ramparts and, deepening his ditches, took up defensive positions. He spoke to Zhang Liang. 'The feudal lords have not adhered to the pact,' he said. 'What shall I do about it?' 'The Chu soldiers are about to be defeated,' he replied, 'but Han Xin and Peng Yue do not yet have any territory allocated to them, so it is surely reasonable for them not to have arrived. If Your Majesty were able to join with them in dividing up the Empire, they could now at once be brought here. But if you are unable to do so at this moment, the outcome cannot yet be known. If you could grant Han Xin everything from Chen eastward right to the sea, and could give Peng Yue what lies north of Suiyang as far as Gucheng, to make sure that each is fighting for himself, then Chu will be easily defeated.'

The King of Han approved this and accordingly sent messengers to inform Han Xin and Peng Yue. 'Combine your forces to attack Chu,' they said. 'When Chu has been defeated, the land to the east of Chen as far as the sea shall be given to the King of Qi, and the land to the north of Suiyang as far as Gucheng shall be given to Chief Minister Peng.' When the messengers arrived, Han Xin and Peng Yue both reported: 'We beg to make our soldiers advance at his moment.' So Han Xin came from Qi and the army of Liu Jia marched together with them from Shouchun. They butchered the people of Chengfu and then came to Gaixia. Grand Marshal Zhou Yin rebelled against Chu and butchered the people of Liu with the aid of the people of Shu. He raised soldiers in Jiujiang, then followed Liu Jia and Peng Yue. They all met at Gaixia, and advanced on King Xiang.

King Xiang had encamped and built ramparts at Gaixia, but his soldiers were few* and the food was all used up. The Han army and the soldiers of the feudal states surrounded him several men deep. At night the Han army was heard on all sides singing the songs of Chu, so King Xiang said in great astonishment: 'Has Han already got the whole of Chu? How many men of Chu there are!' As for King Xiang himself, at night he got up and had a drink in his tent. There was a beautiful woman called Yu, whom he always favoured and took along with him, and a noble steed called Zhui, which he always rode. Thereupon King Xiang sadly sang of his regrets in a song of his own composition:

> My strength plucked up mountains
> And my energies overshadowed the world,
> But the times were not favourable,
> And Zhui will not sally forth again.
> And if Zhui does not sally forth again
> Alas, what can be done?
> Ah Yu! Ah Yu!
> What will become of you?

He sang several verses of the song and the beautiful woman sang in harmony with him. King Xiang's tears streamed down, and those about him all wept, and none could raise their eyes and look up.

King Xiang thereupon mounted his horse and rode off, with 800 and more sturdy fellows riding in attendance under his banner. As soon as night fell they burst through the encirclement and escaped to the south and rode away. So at dawn the Han army became conscious of this, and Cavalry General Guan Ying was ordered to ride off in pursuit of him with 5,000 men. King Xiang crossed the Huai, and only 100 or so horsemen were capable of staying with him. When he reached Yinling, King Xiang suspected that he had lost his way, so he asked a worker in the fields, who, to trick him, told him to go left. He went left and so he got bogged down in a great marsh. For this reason the Han pursuers caught up with him. So King Xiang again led his soldiers off and went eastwards, but when he reached Dongcheng, he in fact had twenty-eight horsemen. The Han horsemen who were in pursuit were several thousand men. King Xiang considered that he could not make a getaway, so he said to his horsemen: 'Eight years have passed from the time when I raised soldiers until now, and I myself have fought in more than seventy battles. Those whom I have confronted have been destroyed, and those whom I have smitten have submitted, and I have never once been defeated and put to flight, and so as paramount prince I have taken possession of all under Heaven. Yet now here I am finally reduced to desperate straits. This is because Heaven is destroying me. It is not because I have done anything wrong in battle. I am certainly resolved to die today, but I would like to fight some quick battles for you, my lords. I shall make a point of being victorious over them three times. For you, my lords, I shall break through the encirclement, I shall decapitate their general, and I shall cut down their banner, so that you, my lords, will understand that Heaven is destroying me, and that it is not that I have done anything wrong in battle.'

Accordingly he divided his horsemen into four groups, facing in all four directions. The Han army encircled them several deep. King Xiang told his horsemen: 'For you gentlemen I will get that one general.' He ordered his horsemen to gallop down in all four directions, and arranged for them to establish three positions on the east of the hill. Then King Xiang gave a great shout and galloped down. The Han army all scattered and then he decapitated one Han general. At this time the Marquis of Chiquan was General of Cavalry and he pursued King Xiang, but King Xiang glared and shouted at him, so that both the Marquis of Chiquan and his horse were startled, and they fled for several *li*. He and his horsemen rendezvoused, forming three different positions, and the Han army did not know which one King Xiang was in, so they divided the army into three and again surrounded them. So King Xiang rode

forth and again decapitated a Han commandant and killed nearly
100 men, and when he gathered his horsemen together again, he
had lost only two of them. So he said to his horsemen: 'What about
it?' The horsemen all prostrated themselves. 'It is just as the Great
King said,' they replied.

Thereupon King Xiang intended to go east and cross over the
River Wu. The headman of the River Wu area, who was waiting
with a moored boat, spoke to King Xiang. 'Although the area east
of the Yangtze is small,' he said, 'it forms a territory of 1,000 *li*
square, and has a population of several hundred thousand, and is
therefore suitable to be ruled by a king. I would like the Great King
to hurry up and cross over. At the moment only your servant has
a boat, but when the Han army arrives, there will be no means of
getting across.' King Xiang smiled. 'Since Heaven is destroying
me,' he said, 'what shall I go across for? Moreover I crossed the
river and went west together with 8,000 young men from east of
the Yangtze, and if I now return without a single man, although
their fathers and elder brothers would make me their king because
they felt pity, how could I bear to look them in the face? Even if they
did not mention it, would I alone not feel shame in my heart?'
Still addressing the headman, he said: 'I know that you, sir, are a
venerable person. I have ridden this steed for five years. He has
no match among those he has confronted, and he once journeyed
1,000 *li* in a single day. I cannot bear to kill him and so I bestow
him upon you.' And so he ordered his horsemen all to dismount
and proceed on foot and join battle brandishing short weapons.
Several hundred men of the Han army were killed by Xiang Yu
alone. He also suffered more than ten wounds on his body. When
he looked round and saw the Han cavalry marshal Lü Matong, he
said: 'Are you not my old friend?' Lü Matong faced him and
pointed him out to Wang Yi. 'This is King Xiang,' he said. King
Xiang then said: 'I hear that Han has placed a reward of 1,000 *jin* and
10,000 households on my head, so I will do you a favour.' Accordingly
he cut his throat and died. Wang Yi picked up his head, and the rest
of the horsemen trampled each other trying to get at King Xiang,
and twenty or thirty killed each other. In the end cavalry attendant
Yang Xi, cavalry marshal Lü Matou, and the palace gentlemen

Lü Sheng and Yang Wu each got one of his limbs. And when the five men fitted his body together, it was all right. Therefore his lands were divided into five: Lü Matou was enfeoffed as Marquis of Zhongshui, Wang Yi was enfeoffed as Marquis of Duyan, Yang Xi was enfeoffed as Marquis of Chiquan, Yang Wu was enfeoffed as Marquis of Wufang, and Lü Sheng was enfeoffed as Marquis of Nieyang.

After King Xiang died, the territory of Chu all fell to Han, except that the people of Lu alone did not submit. So Han led forth the soldiers of the Empire and intended to butcher them, but because of the fact that they had preserved propriety and righteousness and would die a noble death for their lord, they accordingly took King Xiang's head and showed it in Lu, so that the fathers and elder brothers of Lu surrendered. In the beginning King Huai of Chu had enfeoffed Xiang Yu as Duke of Lu and, when it came to the time of his death, Lu was the last to submit, and therefore King Xiang was buried at Gucheng with the ceremony of a Duke of Lu. The King of Han started the mourning for him and, having wept for him, he departed.

All the branches of the Xiang family were not put to death by the King of Han. Indeed he enfeoffed Xiang Bo as Marquis of Sheyang. The Marquis of Tao, the Marquis of Pinggao, and the Marquis of Xuanwu were all of the Xiang family, but they had the surname Liu* bestowed upon them.

The Grand Historiographer said: 'I heard from Master Zhou that Shun's* eyes had double pupils, and I have also heard that Xiang Yu had double pupils too. But Yu was surely not an offshoot of his? How sudden was his rise! When Qin failed in its government, Chen Sheng was at the head of the troubles, and powerful men and local heroes rose up like swarms of bees and competed with each other in incalculable numbers. But although it was not the case that Xiang Yu had the tiniest scrap of land, he took advantage of his skill to rise up from among the dykes and fields, and after three years he commanded five feudal lords* and destroyed Qin. He divided up all under Heaven and enfeoffed kings and marquises, and government emanated from Xiang Yu, who was entitled the Supreme King. Although his status was not maintained until the end, there has never existed such a position since recent antiquity. But when he turned his back on the passes and cherished Chu, drove out the Righteous Emperor, and set himself up, the resentful kings and marquises revolted against him, and things became difficult. He boasted of his own achievements and military offensives, stuck with determination to his own private wisdom, and did not take antiquity as his model. He spoke of the traditions of supreme kingship, but he intended to control all under Heaven by force. But after five years he finally lost his kingdom. When he died at Dongcheng, he still did not wake up and lay the responsibility for his mistakes on himself. Thus surely he was deluded to bring in the words: "Heaven is destroying me, and it is not anything I have done wrong in the use of soldiers." '

8

THE STORY OF THE REBEL CHEN SHENG

Chen Sheng has already been referred to a number of times as one of those who led the rebellions that toppled the Qin Dynasty. An account of his life forms chapter 48 of the Historical Records.

CHEN SHENG was a man of Yangcheng. His courtesy name was She. Wu Guang was a man of Yangxia, and his courtesy name was Shu. When Chen Sheng was young, he was once ploughing with others for hire. He stopped ploughing and went to the top of a hillock and spent a long time there looking dissatisfied. 'Should one of us become rich and noble,' he said, 'there will be no forgetting the rest.' The hired labourers laughed. 'If we are ploughing for hire,' they said, 'how shall we become rich and noble?' 'Alas!' said Chen Sheng with a huge sigh, 'How does a swallow or a sparrow understand the ambition of a wild swan?'

In the seventh month of the first year of the Second Emperor people who were not liable to compulsory service were sent forth to guard Yuyang, and 900 men made camp at Dazexiang. Chen Sheng and Wu Guang had both been due to go, and they had been made heads of the camp. But it happened to rain heavily and the road became impassable, and they reckoned that they were already too late for the appointed time. And if they were too late, by law they should all be executed. Chen Sheng and Wu Guang accordingly plotted together. 'If we desert, we shall die,' they said, 'but if we set great plans in motion, we shall also die. If we are awaiting death, would it be possible for us to die for our country?'

'All under Heaven has for a long time suffered bitterly under Qin,' said Chen Sheng. 'I hear that the Second Emperor is a younger son, who ought not to have been set on the throne. The one who ought to have been set on the throne is in fact Prince Fusu. Because Fusu made frequent remonstrances the Emperor made him take command of troops away from the capital. Now someone has heard that the Second Emperor has put him to death although he is guilty of no crime. The common people hear much of his fine qualities and do not yet know that he has died. Xiang Yan is a Chu general who has had frequent successes and is fond of his officers and soldiers, so that the men of Chu feel sympathetic towards him. Some think he has died, but others think he has deserted. Now if we, with the support of our gang, were falsely to call ourselves Prince Fusu and Xiang Yan, we would become leaders of all under Heaven, for naturally there would be many who would come over to us.'

Wu Guang thought that this was true, so they went to consult the oracle. The diviner was aware that they were indicating their intentions, so he said: 'Your enterprises, gentlemen, will all be completed, and you will have success. But you gentlemen should consult the spirits about it!' Chen Sheng and Wu Guang were delighted but, recalling mention of the spirits, they said: 'This is merely instructing us to make our gang stand in awe of us before we do anything else.' So they wrote on a piece of silk with cinnabar, saying, 'Chen Sheng will be king,' and put it in the belly of a fish which someone had caught in a net. A soldier bought the fish and cooked it to eat, so he found the writing in the belly of the fish with the result that he was certainly amazed at it. He also secretly ordered Wu Guang to go to the shrine in the clump of trees beside the camp, where during the night, with his torch partly concealed under a basket, he howled like a fox and uttered the words: 'Great Chu will rise up and Chen Sheng will become king.' The soldiers all spent the night in terror, and next morning they constantly spoke among themselves, and all pointed and stared at Chen Sheng.

Wu Guang commonly showed his fondness for others, and many of the officers and soldiers would be of service to him. When the commandant was drunk, Guang on several occasions deliberately said that he intended to desert in order to make the commandant furious and cause the latter to humiliate him, so that his gang would be provoked to anger. The commandant did in fact beat Wu Guang, but his sword stuck out; so Guang got up, seized it, and killed the commandant. Chen Sheng went to his assistance and together they killed two other commandants.

They assembled the crowd of followers to give them instructions, saying: 'Because you gentlemen had the bad luck to be rained on, you have all failed to get there on time. Failure to get there on time means you will be sentenced to have your heads cut off. Even supposing that orders were given not to cut off your heads, to be sure six or seven out of ten would die on frontier duty. Moreover if you sturdy fellows do not die, there is nothing more to say; but if you do die you will only be making yourself a great reputation, so it would be far better to have the making of kings, marquises, generals, and ministers!' 'We respectfully receive your commands,' the crowd of followers all said.

Then they falsely took the names of Prince Fusu and Xiang Yan, to fit in with what the people would wish. They bared their right shoulders and proclaimed the Great Chu. An altar was built and they swore a compact, offering the heads of the commandants up in sacrifice. Chen Sheng appointed himself as general and Wu Guang as military commandant.

They attacked Dazexiang and after recruiting further troops, they attacked Qi. Qi was defeated, so they dispatched Ge Ying, a man of Fuli, in command of troops to capture the area east of Qi, and they attacked Zhi, Cus, Ku, Zhe, and Qiao and defeated them all. They recruited soldiers as they went along, and by the time they reached Chen they numbered 600 or 700 chariots, more than 1,000 horsemen, and several tens of thousands of foot-soldiers. When they attacked Chen, neither the Governor nor the magistrates were present. Only an aide of the Governor fought with them at the Qiao gate. He did not conquer them, and indeed the Governor's aide died, and so they entered and occupied Chen. After a few days they sent out an order summoning the village headmen and the powerful local people to come and meet them and make plans for everything which had to be done. The village headmen and the powerful local people all said: 'The general has personally put on hard armour and brandished sharp weapons to attack the unprincipled and punish cruel Qin so as to re-establish the altars of the land and grain of the state of Chu. Through his achievements he ought to become a king.' Chen Sheng accordingly was set up as king, and was called the Magnifier of Chu.

Throughout this period all the provinces and districts which had suffered under Qin officials punished their senior administrators and put them to death in order to collude with Chen Sheng. Then he made Wu Guang an acting king so that all the other generals might go west and attack Xingyang under his supervision.

The next few pages are omitted from this translation since they contain a detailed and complicated account of the internecine struggles of the time and do not make easy reading. The deaths of Chen Sheng and Wu Guang are only briefly noticed: the latter was executed by his fellow-officers because of his arrogance and ignorance of military matters, and Chen Sheng was murdered by his charioteer.

Chen Sheng was king for six months in all, and when he became king he ruled over Chen. An old friend of his, who had once been a hired ploughman with him, heard about this and came to Chen. He knocked on the palace gate and said: 'I want to see Sheng.' The palace gatekeeper wanted to tie him up, but he persisted in explaining himself, so he let him go, but refused to give him access. When the King of Chen came out, he blocked his path and shouted out 'Sheng'. When the King of Chen heard him, he did in fact summon him to interview, and rode back in the carriage together with him. When he entered the palace and saw the furnishings of the halls and residences, the guest said: 'Gosh! Sheng's made a pile since he's been king!' The people of Chu say 'pile' when they mean a lot, so the saying 'Pile Sheng became king' was passed down throughout the world, originating with Chen Sheng. The guest had constant access and made himself increasingly comfortable, and spoke about what the King of Chen used to be like. Someone said to the King of Chen: 'The guest is stupid and ignorant and his simple-minded chatter is weakening your authority.' So the King of Chen cut off his head. All the old friends of the King of Chen took themselves off, and from then on there was nobody who was on close terms with the King of Chen.

The King of Chen appointed Zhu Fang as his Rector* and Hu Wu as his Minister of Faults to take charge of all the officials. When the various generals arrived after capturing territory and there was anything they had done which was not according to instructions, they detained them and brought charges against them, for they regarded vexatious cross-questioning as loyalty. Those whom they disapproved of they did not hand over to the law officers, but they themselves immediately tried them. The King of Chen employed them in good faith, but for this reason all the generals felt no attachment to him, and this is why he was ruined.

Although Chen Sheng was already dead, the marquises, kings, generals, and ministers whom he had appointed and sent forth* in the end wiped out Qin, and the process was initiated by Sheng. In the time of the Han founder, for Chen Sheng's sake thirty families were established at Dang to look after his tomb, and he has enjoyed their sacrifices right up to the present.

The shape of the land and the difficulties of terrain are the means of becoming secure, and weapons and armour, punishments and laws, are the means of becoming well governed; but that is still not yet sufficient to depend on. For the ancient kings regarded humaneness and righteousness as the root and strong frontiers and written laws as the branches and leaves, and surely that is right! I have heard that Master Jia* has proclaimed the following:

Duke Xiao of Qin, relying on the strength of the Xiao Mountains and Hangu Pass, blocked off the territory of Yongzhou, and he and his ministers secured it firmly so as to keep watch on the house of Zhou. For he had the ambition to roll up all under Heaven like a mat, to parcel up everything in the universe, and to put everything within the four seas into a sack, indeed he had the heart to swallow up everything in all directions. During this period Lord Shang was his assistant, and at home he established laws and regulations, ensured that agriculture and weaving were regarded as of fundamental importance, and built up preparations for self-defence; while abroad, having formed alliances, he fought with other states. Thus the men of Qin effortlessly obtained territory outside the area west of the Yellow River.

After Duke Xiao's death, Kings Huiwen, Wu, and Zhaoxiang took over the existing tasks and, employing the policies handed down to them, in the south took Hanzhong, in the west absorbed Ba and Shu, and in the east annexed fertile lands and acquired provinces of strategic importance. The feudal lords were afraid and, holding meetings to agree treaties, made

plans to weaken Qin. They did not begrudge precious vessels or valuable
and fertile territories in order to attract men of valour from everywhere
under Heaven. They joined closely together by making north–south
alliances, and collaborated to form a unity. At this time there was
Mengchang in Qi, Pingyuan in Zhao, Chunshen in Chu, and Xinling in
Wei, and these four lords were all men of intelligence, loyalty, and good
faith. Through their generosity they showed their fondness for others,
and they honoured men of quality and regarded men of valour as important. They formed a north–south alliance, uniting the multitudes of Hann,
Wei, Yan, Zhao, Song, Wey, and Zhongshan. At this time among the men
of valour in the Six States there were people like Ning Yue, Xu Shang,
Su Qin, and Du He, who made plans for them, and the followers of
Qi Ming, Zhou Ju, Chen Zhen, Shao Hua, Lou Huan, Di Jing, Su Li,
and Yue Yi, who saw their plans through, and the likes of Wu Qi, Sun
Bin, Dai Tuo, Er Liang, Wang Liao, Tian Ji, Lian Po, and Zhao She,
who organized their soldiers. With an area ten times that of Qin and with
an army 1,000,000 strong, they gazed upwards at the pass and attacked
Qin. When the men of Qin opened the pass and engaged the enemy, the
armies of the nine states fled and did not dare advance. Without Qin incur-
ring the expenditure of losing a single arrow, all under Heaven had certainly been thrown into difficulties. Thereupon the north–south alliance
broke up and its agreements were nullified, and the states vied with each
other to bribe Qin by ceding territory. With its surplus strength, Qin was
in control of their demise. They pursued the fleeing and drove them
northwards, slaughtering the millions so that their shields floated on a
sea of blood. Taking advantage of the situation, Qin annexed all under
Heaven and split up the mountains and rivers so that the strong states
begged to offer their submission and the weak states came to pay homage.
This brings us to Kings Xiaowen and Zhuangxiang. Because of the brevity
of their reigns the state did not undertake any enterprises.

When we come to the First Emperor, he followed with enthusiasm
the abundant glories of the six reigns, brandished his long whip and
drove all within the universe, swallowed up the two Zhou,* and made
the feudal states disappear. He walked the path of highest honour and
had under his control everything in all directions. He flogged all under
Heaven with his whip, and he overawed and shook all within the four seas.
In the south he took the lands of the various Yue and used them to form
the provinces of Guilin and Xiang, and the lords of the various Yue bowed
their heads and put nooses round their necks, and entrusted their fate to
the subordinate officials. Then Meng Tian was made to go north and

build the Great Wall so as to protect the frontiers, and he pushed back the Xiongnu more than 700 *li*, and the barbarians did not dare to come down south so as to pasture their horses, and their men of valour also did not dare to bend their bows so as to pay back their resentment.

Thereupon he got rid of the ways of the ancient kings, and burnt the sayings of the hundred schools in order to make the black-headed people stupid. He demolished famous city walls, had powerful and eminent people killed, gathered together weapons from all under Heaven and assembled them at Xianyang, where the spears and arrowheads were melted down and cast into a dozen bronze human figures, so as to weaken the people of all under Heaven. Only then did he adopt Hua as his city wall and use the Yellow River as his moat. Indeed he occupied defences of an enormous height from which to look down on unfathomed valleys in order to create security. With skilful generals and strong crossbowmen he guarded the strategic places, and trusty ministers and elite troops deployed their sharp weapons to find out who people were and where they were going. When all under Heaven had been settled, the attitude of mind of the First Emperor was such that he himself thought that the strength of the area within the passes and the 1,000 *li* of metal walls constituted a heritage which his descendants would enjoy as emperors for 10,000 generations.

After the death of the First Emperor, his abundant authority was shaken by strange practices. On the other hand, Chen Sheng was the offspring of a place which had tiny windows and string for door hinges, a day-labourer who had later become a conscript. His talents and abilities were inferior to those of the middling person, and it was not the case that he had the qualities of a Zhongni or a Mo Di* or the riches of a Tao Zhu or Yi Dun. After plodding along in the ranks he found himself among the captains and centurions. After leading soldiers who were weary and scattered, he took command of a host of several hundred and turned round and attacked Qin. Cutting down trees to make weapons and raising bamboo poles to make banners, all under Heaven gathered like a cloud, responded like an echo, and with abundant provisions followed him like a shadow. The powerful and eminent people east of the mountains then rose up together and demolished the house of Qin.

Moreover it is not the case that the Empire was small and weak. The territory of Yongzhou and the stronghold of the Xiao Mountains and the Hangu Pass were just as before. It is not the case that the status of Chen Sheng was more honourable than that of the Lords of Qi, Chu, Yan, Zhao, Hann, Wei, Song, Wey, and Zhongshan. It is not the case that weapons improvised from tool handles are sharper than spears and pikes. It is not the case that a crowd of men conscripted to serve on the frontier is a superior body of men to the armies of nine states. It is not the case that in the technique of either plotting deeply or of showing forethought for the distant future or of moving armies or employing soldiers, he was the equal of the men of valour from former times. Nevertheless their completion of victories was different and their achievements were the opposite of each other. If one tried to compare the authority or measure the strength of the states east of the mountains with those of Chen Sheng, then they would not be fit to be spoken about even in the same year. And yet Qin, with its tiny territory, attained the authority of a 10,000 chariot state, oppressed the eight regions, and made people of the same rank as itself pay homage for more than 100 years. Only then did it treat the whole world as its household and Xiao and Hangu as its palace. But why is it that, when a single individual made trouble, the seven temples* collapsed, and with its ruler dying at men's hands it became a laughing-stock to all under Heaven? Because humaneness and righteousness* were not put into operation, and the qualities needed for attack and defence are different.

EXPLANATORY NOTES

The index may be consulted by those who wish for further information on points of detail.

3 *jin*: this term often occurs when large amounts of money are referred to. Its sense is uncertain since it may mean either 'metal' or 'gold', although the latter is occasionally referred to as 'yellow metal'. Bronze was used commonly in antiquity for currency, originally as a development out of barter objects, especially knives or spades, and gold was employed much more rarely for this purpose. Another difficulty is that there is no formal distinction between singular and plural in the language, and here I have translated 'thousands'. The intention is merely to indicate a very large sum of money.

hostage-son: sons of rulers in antiquity often became 'hostage-sons' in other states in order that they might serve to prevent warfare breaking out between the prince's state of origin and that to which he went as hostage. In this case, as often, the device clearly did not work, and the human shield was left to put up with his fate.

Handan: an important ancient city which had long been the capital of the state of Zhao.

4 *pledges of support*: an important feature of this period was that ambitious princes gathered together bodies of supporters, in some cases providing them with a livelihood.

5 *abundant flowers*: from this strange metaphor it would seem that Lü Buwei is not being credited with much knowledge of the natural world.

tally: half of the tally would be kept by the Crown Prince and half by the Lady. Tallies were often used to guarantee agreements in ancient China. The wording would be embossed on one half of the tally and incised on the other, and the two would need to be fitted together as a guarantee of authenticity. For example, a general in the field might carry one half of a tally, and the other half would be retained at the capital so that a messenger might bear that half to authenticate a message. Such tallies were often in the shape of flattened animals. The material used was often a hard stone other than jade.

time at long last came: it was said that her pregnancy lasted a whole year. There were likely to be special circumstances attending the birth of one who was to attain such greatness: in the case of the founder of the ensuing dynasty, the Han, the sky grew dark, thunder rumbled and lightning flashed, and a scaly dragon hovered over his mother just before she became pregnant.

6 *posthumous name*: it was the common practice in historical writings for rulers to be referred to by their posthumous names, which were appropriately grandiloquent. Xiaowen means 'filial and cultured'.

6 *uncle*: an echo of the fact that Guan Zhong, the celebrated minister of Duke Huan of Qi, who reigned in the seventh century BC and was the first of the 'paramount princes', was addressed by Duke Huan as 'uncle'.

Lord Xinling: the four aristocrats mentioned here are the most famous princes of the third century BC who gathered together groups of supporters, as described in the above note on 'pledges of support'. They were reputed to have gathered as many as 3,000 supporters each, who sometimes served as a kind of private army. It is for this reason that I have often translated the difficult word *shi* as 'men of action'. But the word *shi*, which could be translated consistently in my version of the *Analects* (World's Classics, 1993) as 'public servants', is very wide-ranging in meaning in the *Historical Records* and encompasses men of all manner of initiatives and achievements. Sometimes there is more emphasis on intellectual accomplishments, as in the case of the group Lü Buwei assembled. He obviously wished to improve the cultural reputation of Qin, which was looked down on by the other states.

Xun Qing: he flourished between *c.*298 and 238 BC and was the third great Confucian thinker and teacher (after Master Kong himself and Master Meng) and the first to produce his own book. The reference to books spreading 'throughout the world' involved the copying of manuscripts since this was long before the invention of printing.

7 *Springs and Autumns of Lü*: this eclectic work survives but, unfortunately, has not yet been translated into English. A German version by Richard Wilhelm (*Frühling und Herbst des Lü Bu Wei*) was published in 1928.

First Emperor: King Zheng is generally referred to thus, although from 246 to 221 BC, when he unified China, he was merely king of Qin. However, Zhou was plainly finished and, in order to fill the gap and preserve the fiction of continuity, the Qin Dynasty is sometimes taken as dating from as early as 255 BC.

seventh year: although this is described as the seventh year of the First Emperor, it actually refers to the seventh year of his rule over Qin (i.e. 240 BC), as explained in the previous note.

8 *Queen Dowager Xia*: i.e. the concubine of Lord Anguo who was the mother of Zichu, who had later become the King of Qin and was known posthumously as King Zhuangxiang. She wanted the world to know that, concubine though she was, she was the wife of one ruler of Qin and mother of another.

Shu: a remote semi-barbarian region in present-day Sichuan, which had come under Qin control in the late fourth century BC and flourished as an independent state in the third and tenth centuries AD.

9 *Grand Historiographer*: Sima Qian generally concludes chapters of the *Historical Records* with comments similar to this, sometimes merely summarizing the information given in the biography and moralizing about it and sometimes providing additional information. There is a puzzle over the use of the expression the 'Grand Historiographer' since it would have been immodest of Sima Qian to have referred to himself thus. I have used the

conventional translation although, as explained in the Introduction, the book was written before the duties of this official were primarily historiographical.

Supreme One: emperors are sometimes referred to as *shang*, meaning 'above' or 'superior'. Translators have not normally differentiated between this and *huang-di*, meaning 'emperor', but it seems to me better to do so and I have therefore rendered the expression by 'the Supreme One'.

the man of reputation: this refers to a quotation from *Analects* 12. 20: 'The man of reputation assumes an air of humaneness although his conduct belies it.'

11 *Wey*: there are two states in pre-imperial China romanized as Wei, both of which are mentioned in this chapter. To distinguish the two I have used 'Wey' for the old state, which was very weak in the third century BC, and 'Wei' for the state sometimes known as 'Liang', which was one of the three successor states of Jin.

bo: the board-game which is known as *weiqi* in modern Chinese or *go* in Japanese. The importance of these seemingly irrelevant stories becomes clear at the end of the biography when Lu expresses his appreciation of Jing Ke's qualities.

12 *King Zheng of Qin was born in Zhao*: he was, of course, the one destined to become the First Emperor of China. His birth in the state of Zhao and the machinations of Lü Buwei in this connection are alluded to in Ch. 1.

three successor states of Jin: the important states of Hann, Wei, and Zhao. This was the time when the Qin unification of China was imminent and even the remote state of Yan in the north-east was under threat.

all under Heaven: the phrase *tian-xia* ('under Heaven'), used nominally and conventionally translated 'all under Heaven', is commonly used in the literature of ancient China, but it is particularly difficult to render at this time because it is beginning to have its later common meaning of 'empire'. I have therefore sometimes translated it thus, but have retained 'all under Heaven' when it occurs in the old-fashioned sense.

13 *River Yi*: the boundary of Yan. He is referring in a roundabout way to Yan territory.

Guan and Yan: Guan Zhong and Yan Ying were powerful ancient ministers in the service of Qi which, like Yan, was a state in the north-east. Guan Zhong was the power behind the throne of Duke Huan, the first of the paramount princes. He flourished in the seventh century BC, while Yan Ying operated in the sixth century BC. They are referred to here because they were paragons of political wisdom. The citation of historical precedent is a common ploy in ancient Chinese argumentation.

Xiongnu: the powerful northern nomadic people often wrongly identified with the Huns.

14 *mat*: it was customary in antiquity for the Chinese to sit on mats. *Juxi*, the modern Chinese word for 'chairman' (as in 'Chairman Mao'), means 'mat-master'.

15 *cut his throat and died*: this may seem excessive, but one is reminded of Hou Sheng, who similarly committed suicide precisely when he calculated that his master was bound to meet his death at the hands of Qin. This timely act meant that he would be able to serve his master in the next world, although old age had prevented him from attending him in this. (His story is told in chapter 77 of the *Historical Records*.) Another example of honourable suicide comes later in this chapter.

16 *north—south alliance*: this type of alliance, designed to thwart the ambitions of Qin, which lay in the west, is frequently mentioned in these pages.

man of action: this is clearly a place where 'man of action' is a better translation of *shi* than anything which smacks of intellectual, social, or moral superiority.

Cao Mo: another of the 'assassins' featured in this biography. He was a general of Lu who, by threatening the famous Duke Huan of Qi with a dagger, succeeded in securing the restoration of certain territory which Lu had had to concede to Qi.

17 *Dukang*: an area of fertile and therefore desirable land within the state of Yan.

clasping his wrist: a gesture of determination.

18 *white mourning clothes*: white is the colour of mourning in China. The wearing of such clothes would be appropriate if Jing Ke were doomed, and it was common practice to try to ward off ill-fortune by preparing for the worst.

stirring tune: the text adds 'in the key of *yu*'.

19 *Son of Heaven*: a reference to the King of Qin, which is premature since he has not yet succeeded in establishing the Empire, which would have entitled him to such a grandiose label. Notice also Jing Ke's cheeky implication that he himself was quite used to having audience with the Great King.

20 *yi*: it is not easy to tell what weight this represents. The general view is that it normally amounts to about 20 ounces, but 4,000 ounces of gold would be a very large sum indeed.

city of Ji: the capital city of Yan.

21 *Liaodong*: literally 'east of the Liao'; an area with that name still exists in China.

River Yan: a river in Liaodong, written with a different character from that used to write the state of Yan.

August Emperor: this is explained in more detail in Ch. 5.

22 *Heaven . . . horns*: according to one version of this story, the King of Qin had refused to let him return home unless these unnatural occurrences took place. Prince Dan's success in bringing them about secured his release.

they told it to me: this seems extremely improbable since the event is supposed to have taken place before the unification of China in 221 BC and Sima Qian was not born until 145 BC, unless Xia Wuju had managed to discover the secret of longevity which had eluded so many contemporary charlatans.

From Cao Mo to Jing Ke: the five 'assassins' whose stories are recorded in this chapter.

23 *Six States*: the six major states—Hann, Wei, Zhao, Chu, Yan, and Qi— all of which were defeated by Qi in the decade 230–221 BC.

10,000 chariots: major states were sometimes referred to as 10,000 char- iot states. At this time of turmoil itinerant advisers who went from state to state advocating their solutions to the political problems of the day were prominent and Li Si sees himself becoming one of these.

title of emperor: the Chinese is *di*, a title rich in historical and religious associations, used for example in connection with the ancient sage-kings Yao and Shun. The title *wang* (king) had lost its prestige since it had been usurped by rulers of the feudal states. It is, of course, inappropriate to credit Li Si with such a statement, since he cannot have known of the King of Qin's intentions. This is a good illustration of the artificiality of the speeches in Sima Qian.

24 *lack of purposive activity*: my translation for the Daoist virtue of *wu wei*, which Li Si specifically rejects.

palace gentleman: a candidate for office who served a probationary period at court while awaiting recommendation and appointment.

area of the Six States: the text actually says 'annex the Six States', but this is anachronistic. What is meant is the area occupied by the six major states at the time of speaking.

virtue: the word *de* is very difficult to translate and I have often simply adopted the conventional translation which is 'virtue'. What is intended here is the store of magico-moral power which dynasties were thought to possess at their commencement by virtue of the fact that they had won the Mandate of Heaven.

five hegemons: there are frequent references in ancient literature to the five hegemons or paramount princes, who acted as leaders of the alliance of northern states which was formed in the seventh century BC as the Zhou Dynasty grew weak. Different lists of these five are given in different authorities, but in fact only Duke Huan of Qi and Duke Wen of Jin clearly fulfilled this role. Duke Mu of Qin, for example, was never actually paramount prince.

six reigns: i.e. the reigns preceding that of King Zheng of Qin, lasting from 360 to 246 BC.

25 *construction of drainage and irrigation channels*: this matter is discussed in greater detail in the chapter on rivers and canals, the relevant part of which is translated in Ch. 6. This was a perfectly sensible scheme, and the belief that it was a ruse to cause dissension emanated both from the resentment of the labourers employed and from the jealousy of the aristocrats at the engagement of a foreigner to organize this major work.

expulsion of aliens: the decree for the expulsion of aliens dates from 237 BC, nine years after the scheme organized by Zheng Guo, so it may in fact have been prompted by the revolt of the alien Lao Ai in 238 BC. Moreover the alien Lü Buwei was discredited in 237 BC. The following paragraph shows how four successful rulers of Qin obtained great benefit from the employment of aliens. The detail is not always accurate, nor are the arguments always cogent.

25 *li*: about a third of a mile. 'A thousand *li*' indicates a rough order of magnitude of approximately 1,000 *li* square.

Yan: like Ying, a very important city in the state of Chu, not to be confused with the state called Yan, which is written with a different character.

26 *jade from the Kun Mountains*: the purpose of this paragraph is to show how the Qin court made use of goods imported from remote places. The reader may be surprised to discover that a section on the import of alien goods is considered relevant to the argument concerning the expulsion of aliens, but in ancient Chinese thought Heaven, Earth, and Man were regarded as closely interacting entities. The interrelatedness of Heaven, Earth, and Man is also well illustrated in the following paragraph.

women of Zhao: this state was most famous for feminine beauty. It is difficult to find accurate equivalents of the adjectives used to describe the women of Zhao: 'charming' is a translation of a word used in the first piece in the *Book of Songs* to describe a bride.

27 *the Five Emperors and the Three Kings*: the Five Emperors were legendary figures from the third millennium BC, and the Three Kings refers to the founders of the Xia, Yin, and Zhou Dynasties.

28 *he did not set up . . . kings*: a conspicuous passage showing Sima Qian writing from hindsight. He knew that the Han founder had set up relatives in their own principalities, and this had led to the revolt of the seven imperial princes in 154 BC.

Scholars of Broad Learning: the body of seventy court scholars. The word is sometimes translated 'academicians', but in my versions of the names of offices and other technical terms I have tended to try to convey the flavour of the original.

Qi: this state was a traditional centre of Confucianism, so Chunyu Yue argues in favour of the importance of the family. The word 'remonstrated' is often used to describe a speech made to a ruler. The ruler's task was to take advice and heed remonstrance, but to take decisions himself.

Tian Chang or the six ministers: this refers to two important episodes in Chinese history: the murder of the Qi ruler in 481 BC by Tian Chang, followed by his usurpation of the throne; and the contention for the control of Jin, which resulted in its being divided up into Hann, Wei, and Zhao in 403 BC.

29 *get rid of it*: a reference to one of the most famous events in ancient Chinese history, the 'burning of the books' in 213 BC. The works referred to are the earliest collections of poetry and historical documents, together with the philosophical and other literature covered by the 'hundred schools'.

(Readers may recall the famous Maoist saying 'Let a hundred flowers bloom, let a hundred schools of thought contend.') The purpose was not to exterminate learning, but to monopolize it by ensuring that copies were available only to academicians working in the imperial library. Unfortunately, when this burnt down in the conflagration at the end of the Qin Dynasty, a sad loss of ancient literature occurred, so that during the Former Han Dynasty works had to be restored either from hidden copies or the memories of aged scholars.

tortoiseshell and milfoil: the former was the more prestigious method. Heat was applied to a tortoiseshell and divinations made in accordance with the shape of the cracks that appeared. Milfoil divination depended on the number of sticks of milfoil.

standardized documents: the text here seems not to refer to the standardization of the script, which did occur at this time, but to the standardization of bureaucratic practices.

Xun Qing: the quotation given here does not occur in the present text of his writings.

when things reach their peak they decline: a succinct statement of the cyclical views of history then prevailing in China.

30 *seventh month*: this comes after the tenth month (which starts the preceding paragraph) simply because the Qin year started with the tenth month of the old Zhou calendar and retained the old Zhou numbering.

31 *Tang and Wu*: in fact they did not kill their rulers. Tang, the founder of the Yin Dynasty, exiled the tyrant Jie; and Wu, the Zhou founder, forced the tyrant Zhou (written with a different character from the dynastic Zhou) to commit suicide. It is not known to what the parricide Lord of Wey in the next sentence refers.

Different localities each...propriety: Zhao Gao does not argue consistently from the Legalist viewpoint. This is a rather anti-Legalist sentiment.

great occurrence: the First Emperor's death.

32 *at Huhai's place*: this seems to be a lie since we were earlier told that they were at Zhao Gao's place.

brush and scraper clerk: in antiquity a knife was used to scrape out mistakes made on wooden tablets. The brush was the normal writing implement.

33 *give offence*: i.e. by blaming or criticizing you.

constant laws: this again completely contradicts Legalism, which does believe in constant laws. Hereabouts Zhao Gao is indulging in highfalutin waffle in order to try to win Li Si over.

34 *three events*: these are famous in Chinese history. The first refers to the internecine struggles in Jin following the death of Duke Xian in 652 BC; in the second episode Duke Huan's brother was finally executed, and it was said that when Duke Huan himself died in 643 BC he remained

unburied for two months, but in fact this story may have arisen because of the discrepancy of two months in the dating systems used in the *Zuo Tradition*; thirdly, Zhou, the tyrannical last ruler of the Yin Dynasty, is supposed to have cut open the heart of his kinsman Bi Gan to see whether it was true that the sage's heart had seven orifices.

a Kong or a Mo: Zhao Gao is depicted as showing admiration for Kong (Confucius) and Mo (founder of the Mohist school), rather than Legalist worthies. It is interesting also to notice that the pine, which commonly symbolizes longevity in later works of art, is already used as a symbol of long life. (Another interpretation takes the words for 'lofty pine' separately, as referring to two obscure legendary individuals known as 'Lofty' and 'Pine'.)

35 *prolong Our allotted span*: the First Emperor was certainly keen to obtain the elixir of immortality, but this sentence does not seem to fit in with the rest of the letter.

Meng Tian: Zhao Gao had a grudge against the Mengs because he had once been condemned to death by Meng Tian's brother Meng Yi. He received a special pardon from the First Emperor.

36 *Meng Tian is dead*: this is in conflict with the biography of Meng Tian, where Meng Yi is said to have held a civil post and to have been executed before the death of Meng Tian.

involve others: the Legalist system of mutual responsibility implied that relatives should keep an eye on each other's conduct and should be held responsible for their kinsmen's crimes.

37 *Mount Li*: the site of the tomb of the First Emperor. The so-called 'terracotta warriors' excavated in 1974 and now one of the main tourist attractions of the People's Republic of China were intended to serve as defenders of this tomb.

38 *area east of the mountains*: i.e. the area east of the mountains in which the strategic Hangu Pass, which commanded the eastern approaches to Qin, was situated.

Master Han: the Legalist philosopher Han Feizi.

3 feet off the ground: already in ancient China grand buildings were raised high above ground level. The practice persisted in modern times, as for example in the Forbidden City in Beijing. The Yao referred to is the legendary sage-emperor.

Yu: the legendary founder of the Xia Dynasty who is famous for having tamed the flood that afflicted China in his day.

39 *supervision and allocating responsibility*: these key techniques in the Legalist system form the topic of this somewhat turgid memorial. If a ruler is fully capable of putting the techniques into operation, the Empire in effect becomes self-governing. Hence, as the memorial says a little later on, 'the sovereign alone governs in the Empire and yet there are none whom he governs'.

Master Shen: the Legalist philosopher Shen Buhai, who lived in the fourth century BC. Only fragments of his writings have survived.

41 *Lou Ji*: it is not known for certain who he was, but he is clearly quoted as a symbol of athleticism, just as Robber Zhi is the classic exponent of theft. Mount Tai, the famous sacred mountain in Shandong, is much higher than mentioned. These particular examples do not seem very pertinent to the preceding argument, unlike the case of Robber Zhi, which is cited to illustrate the effectiveness of severe punishments for light offences.

men who are . . . righteous: i.e. men who possess Confucian virtues.

43 *the mysterious one*: although this had once been a first-person pronoun with a more general provenance, it came to be reserved for imperial use, the nuance being apparent from this passage.

45 *all-in wrestling*: these games were abolished in 44 BC and the precise nature of them was forgotten in antiquity. They originated from military exercises and were probably a sort of wrestling.

Han Yi: this episode is otherwise unknown, but the usurpations of Zihan and Tian Chang are attested elsewhere.

'What!' . . . Generation: it seems that Li Si was granted an audience after all, although at the beginning of the previous paragraph we were told that he could not obtain an audience because of the Emperor's preoccupation with entertainments.

We: used here to render the imperial first-person pronoun *zhen*, 'the mysterious one'.

46 *Jie killed Guan Longfeng*: Jie, the wicked last ruler of the Xia Dynasty, put the worthy Guan Longfeng to death; Wu Zixu was ordered to commit suicide after giving wise but unwelcome advice.

47 *the reason why Si did not die*: Sima Qian himself submitted to castration rather than death, in his case because he attached importance to the completion of his historical writings.

49 *Xiang Liang*: one of the anti-Qin rebel leaders and uncle of Xiang Yu, alias King Xiang (see Ch. 7). According to that account, he and the future founder of the Han Dynasty, the Governor of Pei, had inflicted a heavy defeat on Qin forces, and Li You had had his head cut off.

five punishments: accounts vary, but branding and the amputation of various parts of the body are generally mentioned.

third degree: a vague term to cover a concept that is differently explained in different contexts. Literally it means 'wipe out the three clans', and it may refer to the father's, mother's, and wife's clans.

Chief Minister from the Palace: this title was given to the Chief Minister when he was an eunuch.

presented a deer . . . horse: a *locus classicus* for a ruler being duped by an all-powerful minister. A somewhat different version of the story is given in Ch. 5.

49 *Shanglin*: a famous imperial park just outside the capital.

50 *son-in-law*: later in Chinese history it was common for powerful eunuchs to adopt children and set up domestic establishments. Presumably this is what has happened here, rather than that he has become an eunuch after becoming a father.

younger brother: Ch. 5 gives a very different account of the relationship. It says that he was a nephew of Second Generation, which would make him the First Emperor's grandson. Precocious though the imperial family doubtless were, Ziying could hardly have had that relationship with the First Emperor and at the same time had children mature enough to be worthy of consultation.

the Wu Pass: the southern pass into Qin. (The Governor of Pei, as already mentioned, later became the founder of the Han Dynasty.)

51 *Six Classics*: the six works that later formed the nucleus of the Confucian Classics.

Zhou and Shao: the Dukes of Zhou and Shao were much-revered figures who helped to establish the Zhou Dynasty.

53 *south of the Yellow River*: area south of the river when it takes an east–west course in what is now Inner Mongolia.

54 *Zhao Gao*: the Zhao surname was that of the royal family of the state of that name.

King of Qin: by this time he had already become First Emperor, so this usage and the next are both anachronistic.

56 *three rulers lost their states*: these are all episodes dating from the last few pre-imperial years: the events leading to the destruction of the state of Zhao in 228 BC; the attempted assassination of the King of Qin leading to the destruction of the state of Yan as recounted in our second chapter; and, finally, Hou Sheng's surrender of the Qi army to Qin in 221 BC, which signalled the Qin assumption of the Empire. (Note that King Xi rather than Crown Prince Dan is here described as the employer of Jing Ke.)

bestow death: i.e. give opportunity to commit suicide, instead of being executed.

57 *False*: the posthumous titles of rulers are normally flattering. Mu means 'majestic' but another way of writing the name can be used and this sometimes means 'false'. Hence this bogus piece of etymology.

58 *threes and fives*: i.e. one must sort people out. No such quotation is to be found in this section of the *Book of Documents*.

61 *King of Hann*: this paragraph lists some of the events leading to the successful unification of China by Qin.

63 *Ten Thousandth Generation*: one of the most ironic moments in history, since Second Generation had been on the throne for only a few years when the whole edifice came tumbling down.

Five Powers: according to this theory, the Five Powers (sometimes known as Five Elements, but in the Chinese *wu de*, using the *de* which is often translated as 'virtue') were each in turn associated with a new dynasty. Zhou was associated with the Power of Fire, which had to be succeeded by the Power of Water, since water overcomes fire. By the same rationale, the other Powers would succeed in the series earth, wood, metal. There was much speculation concerning this doctrine, and differences of opinion as to which power should be associated with which historical period. There was also an elaborate system of correspondences between powers, colours, numbers, and so on. The colour black and number six, which are referred to in the text, were associated with the Power of Water.

64 *1,000 piculs in weight*: a huge weight, since a picul is what a man can carry.

standardized the characters: in this version of the reforms the text speaks of the standardization of the script rather than of bureaucratic practice. The standardization of the axle length of carriages may appear bizarre or possibly a concession to numerology, but it may have seemed prudent to have wheel-ruts a standard size, especially in loess country.

65 *beautiful women, bells, and drums*: possession of harems and the means of providing musical entertainment were the prizes of conquest which symbolized the unification. This is a clear statement of the commonly expressed view that the main purpose of political power was to ensure that one enjoyed all the pleasures of life.

feng and shan sacrifices: important sacrifices performed by emperors when they felt their authority was secure. Their importance is reflected in the fact that Sima Qian's chapter devoted to religious practices is named after these sacrifices (see Ch. 6).

fifth-rank grandee: in making his horse a consul Caligula did at least confer the honour on an animate object!

stone tablet: the inscription is in the form of four-character phrases with a rhyme at the end of the third of these phrases. In this translation the breaks are indicated by two commas and a full stop. The language is traditional and grandiose and makes little reference to Legalist principles.

66 *inscription extolling the virtue of Qin*: the structure of this inscription is different from the earlier one, with each 'sentence' consisting of two instead of three four-character phrases; but the sentiment is much the same. The last part of the inscription is in prose.

68 *six directions*: up and down, as well as north, south, east, and west.

69 *Zhou cauldrons*: these cauldrons, allegedly made by the sage-king Yu, had long been recognized as symbols of dynastic power, and that is why their recovery justified such expenditure of manpower. In fact the text of this chapter records earlier that the cauldrons 'entered Qin' on the collapse of the Zhou regime in 256 BC. This has led to some speculation that only one of these precious vessels was lost in the river, but it seems wiser to believe in the inconsistency of Sima Qian.

69 *bandits*: a somewhat muffled allusion to an attempt on the life of the First Emperor by Zhang Liang, who was determined to take vengeance for the demise of his own state of Hann; but as recounted elsewhere in the biography of this worthy (chapter 55 of the *Historical Records*) he made an attack with the aid of a hired strong man, using a massive iron bludgeon, but failed to hit the right carriage.

71 *the Felicitous and Equable*: this festival had previously been known as *la*, but the First Emperor decided to make the change when he discovered that it had had this much grander name during the Yin Dynasty.

72 *Hu*: the most obvious interpretation of this prediction was that it referred to the Hu, or northern barbarians, who were accordingly attacked. The real menace, however, was the Emperor's favourite son and eventual successor, Huhai, the first syllable of whose name was written with the same character.

men who had . . . traders: this apparently motley collection of recruits consisted of those who had run away to avoid taxation or labour service, as well as those who suffered the indignity of living with their wives' families because they had not the wherewithal to set up on their own, while the lowly position of the third group in a society which condemned the market-place may be readily understood.

73 *Tian Chang*: these events and the speeches about them have already been referred to in the parallel passage in Ch. 3.

74 *Your servant requests . . . burnt*: a fuller version of this episode than we have previously encountered, with a reference to the 'burning of the books'.

75 *500 paces*: the dimensions here are hugely exaggerated, and the rest of this passage is not to be taken too literally. This is why I have used the fancy word 'myriad' rather than '10,000' in my translation, since the English word can, like its Chinese equivalent, be used rather vaguely.

Encampment: one of the twenty-eight heavenly mansions into which the heavens were divided by astronomers. The Apex of Heaven is also an area of the heavens rather than an individual star.

76 *hangings, bells, drums, and beautiful women*: again this passage perhaps has more in common with fiction than history, and one is reminded of the scandalous stories which appeared in popular literature about Emperor Yang of the Sui Dynasty.

78 *Master Kong*: this reference to Master Kong (Confucius) illustrates the difficulty of understanding how much Sima Qian, writing a century later, has put his own gloss on events: the speeches must, of course, be inventions to dramatize the situation, but although the reference to the law chimes in with the Legalist aspirations mentioned elsewhere, the reference to Master Kong is more suspect and may have been written from the Han Dynasty viewpoint.

mansion of the Heart: another of the twenty-eight heavenly mansions into which the sky was divided.

79 *consulted the tortoiseshell*: plainly the Emperor is perturbed by the series of strange events and is afraid that they foretell his imminent death.

guichou: occasionally the names of days are referred to using a sexagenary cycle.

80 *system of laws*: there is some reference to Legalist principles in this inscription, especially here and in the preceding sentence.

name: notice the reference to the doctrine of the rectification of names, which implies that one cause of chaos is the fact that things no longer bear their proper names.

82 *biography of Li Si*: Ch. 3.

Mount Li: an interesting description of the First Emperor's tomb follows. Since the tomb has not yet been excavated, there is no possibility of comparing this account with the actuality.

87 *report the rebellion*: one of the great weaknesses of the Chinese imperial system was that messengers did not dare to bring bad news. This occurred conspicuously, for example, in the unexpected overthrow of the Ming Dynasty in the seventeenth century.

90 *deer*: compare the parallel passage in Ch. 3.

95 *red bird*: an omen that encouraged King Wu when he attacked the wicked last emperor of the Yin Dynasty.

96 *kept totally secret*: when this sacrifice was performed by Emperor Wu of the Former Han Dynasty, the secrecy was preserved by ensuring that the Emperor was accompanied to the top of Mount Tai by only one individual, who was afterwards conveniently smitten by a violent illness, which caused him to die on the same day.

97 *Linzi*: the capital of the state of Qi. One of the meanings of the character for Qi is 'navel'. The following sentence, which is in parentheses, is wrongly situated in the original text.

Chi You: a legendary figure who was fond of fighting. Sacrifices had to be made at Chi You's tomb.

Master Cou: Cou Yan, whose name is particularly associated with theorizing about the Five Powers. Wei and Xuan were fourth-century BC rulers of Qi.

99 *passed away*: earlier accounts of the First Emperor's death occur in Chs. 3 and 5. It seems particularly sad and rather pointed that his death should be briefly mentioned here just after an account of his searches for the elixir of immortality.

100 *Treasures of Chen*: these objects are said to have come into the possession of Duke Wen, an eighth-century BC ruler of Qin. They were said to have looked like cockerels and uttered a screeching sound which made the local hens respond, even in the middle of the night.

102 *40,000 qing ... one zhong per mou*: a *qing*, which is the equivalent of just over 11 acres, consists of 100 *mou*. A *zhong* is approximately equivalent to 8 litres.

104 *clan will be wiped out*: the Chinese simply has a very potent verbal use of the one word 'clan'—'we shall be clanned'.

8 feet: the Chinese foot was equivalent to about three-quarters of an English foot.

Kuaiji: a large province established by the Qin in the far east of China, in present-day Jiangsu and Zhejiang provinces. The Yangtze flows in a north-easterly direction near its mouth: hence the region beyond the Yangtze is referred to as the 'area west of the Yangtze'.

105 *King Chen*: the rebel Chen Sheng, who had by this time already become a king, a distinction he held for a mere six months (see Ch. 8).

106 *Huai*: this important river would be the next hurdle Xiang Liang had to cross in his march towards the Qin heartlands.

Pengcheng: an important city which was to become capital of the reconstituted kingdom of Chu established by the Xiangs.

Zhang Han: the main Qin general.

Governor of Pei: the future First Emperor of the Han Dynasty, who has already been encountered, features prominently in this chapter. Pei was his home town. He put its Qin governor to death and styled himself Pei-gong, which has been translated Governor, Duke, or Lord, of Pei.

107 *King Huai*: he reigned over Chu from 327 to 298 BC, when his reign terminated because he was tricked into Qin and held prisoner there. He died in Qin in 296 BC. As we shall see shortly, his grandson, who was living as a commoner, was set up as King of Chu, and also came to be known as King Huai.

King of Qi: hereabouts there is much complicated detail. The main theme, however, is that the rebellion is now taking the form of the reconstitution of ancient kingdoms, first Chu and now Qi.

108 *Li You*: the son of Li Si, whose death is also referred to in Ch. 3.

Song Yi: a Chu general who plays an important part in later events.

109 *Julu*: an important strategic city which had formerly been in the state of Zhao.

111 *soldiers of Chu*: this paragraph vividly describes the acme of the power of Chu and Xiang Yu.

carriage-shaft gates: we are here reminded of the Boer laager.

112 *Bai Qi was a Qin general*: another typical passage of argumentation from historical precedent.

113 *solitary one*: this expression was commonly used by rulers of themselves, in reference to their having lost their fathers. The solution of a break-up into independent kingdoms is here being openly advocated.

waste of Yin: the old Yin Dynasty capital at Anyang is often referred to thus.

Qin armies: i.e. the troops of Qin which had surrendered with Zhang Han.

114 *Ziying*: he was, of course, the relative of the First Emperor who reigned for a mere forty-six days at the end of the Qin Dynasty.

115 *Great King*: i.e. the Governor of Pei.

116 *Xiang Zhuang*: a cousin of Xiang Yu.

117 *That King of Qin*: i.e. the First Emperor. Later 'the Great King' refers to Xiang Yü.

119 *three months*: this long conflagration was the cause of the great loss of literature which, by the events of 213 BC, had been monopolized for the use of court scholars.

make himself a king: become ruler of a kingdom, as opposed to someone who merely held the grandiose title of king.

120 *the Empire was divided up*: the important historical decision behind this and the preceding paragraph is that Xiang Yu saw the future in terms of a proliferation of small territories in alliance with each other rather than as a centralized empire.

122 *Emperor Hui and Yuan of Lu*: the two children of the King of Han, who was destined to become the First Emperor of the Han Dynasty. This is a conspicuous example of how Sima Qian provides the names of people as they were known in his own time. The emperor posthumously known as Emperor Hui reigned from 194 to 187 BC. His sister was known as Yuan of Lu.

the Supreme Duke and the Empress Lü: the King of Han's father and wife.

Xiao He: a very famous early Han politician, who was the Han founder's first chief minister and played a prominent part in the foundation of the dynasty.

Ao Granary: a key strategic facility, storing grain from the rich plain between the Yellow and Huai Rivers. This passage illustrates its importance.

123 *yellow-canopied carriage*: i.e. the royal carriage.

124 *Wei Bao*: he had formerly been King of Wei.

127 *done Xiang Liang a favour*: this episode has already been reported near the beginning of the chapter.

pact with Han: notice this agreement, dividing the Empire up between the two forces. The arrangement was not to survive for long.

128 *Lord . . . State*: this puzzling remark in parentheses does not occur in the parallel in the *History of the Former Han Dynasty* and may not be authentic.

129 *soldiers were few*: we are now coming to the dramatic denouement of the whole story. In reading this chapter sharpness of sight is necessary to enable one to extract the nuggets of historical truth from the rich seam of fantasy. There is, of course, other relevant material in the *History of the Former Han Dynasty* as well as in other parts of the *Historical Records*, but space precludes reference being made to it here.

132 *surname Liu*: i.e. the Han Dynasty imperial surname.

Shun's: i.e. those of the legendary sage-emperor so called.

five feudal lords: this refers to the reconstituted states of Qi, Yan, Zhao, Hann, and Wei. The next sentence alludes to Xiang Yu's policy of dividing the Empire up into small states. The summary also wisely remarks on Xiang Yu's fatal decision to retreat from the centre and go back to Chu.

138 *Rector*: the terms 'Rector' and 'Minister of Faults' are not part of the normal panoply of official titles.

139 *appointed and sent forth*: Chen Sheng's role is much exaggerated, but the fact that he initiated the rebellion was recognized by the Han founder as indicated.

Master Jia: this chapter does not conclude with the usual summary from the Grand Historiographer. Instead there is a quotation from a famous essay entitled 'The Faults of Qin', written by Jia Yi early in the Former Han period. This essay occurs elsewhere in the *Historical Records*, but is included here as an appropriate summary and conclusion to the book. The important events summarized will be familiar from earlier references, so detailed notes have not been provided.

140 *two Zhou*: this term is used because the Zhou Dynasty was divided into two, the eastern and western Zhou, when the capital had to be removed from the Xi'an to the Luoyang area in the eighth century BC.

141 *a Zhongni or a Mo Di*: a reference to the founders of the Confucian and Mohist schools.

142 *seven temples*: Sons of Heaven had that number of ancestral temples.

humaneness and righteousness: i.e. Confucian principles.

INDEX

References to the map are in **bold** type.